THE RISE OF ROME

How To Explain It

PROBLEMS IN EUROPEAN CIVILIZATION

THE RISE OF ROME

How To Explain It

EDITED WITH AN INTRODUCTION BY

David Hood

CALIFORNIA STATE COLLEGE

LONG BEACH

D. C. HEATH AND COMPANY

A Division of Raytheon Education Company

Lexington, Massachusetts

CONTENTS

INTRODUCTION

WHY did Rome rise to rule an Empire to which all roads led and all Mediterranean kings bowed? For over two thousand years thoughtful men have pondered this question. Rome's meteoric rise challenges historians to speculation and debate, and no final explanation for Rome's success has yet been found. However, insofar as the modern world is the heir of the ancient, we must understand Rome to fully understand ourselves, and so we must consider the problem of Rome's rise to power.

Rome's expansion was spectacular. Beginning as a small farming village in central Italy, Rome proceeded to master the Mediterranean. Under Etruscan domination from the legendary founding of the city, the Romans expelled their Etruscan overlords in 509 B.C. and formed a federation of Latin allies for mutual defense. By 290 Rome had unified the hill tribes of central and southern Italy under her leadership; by 270 she had brought the Greek cities of the south into her federation. From 264 to 201 Rome fought two successful wars with Carthage (until then the undisputed mistress of the western Mediterranean), annexed Sicily and Spain, and made firm diplomatic commitments throughout the western part of the ancient world. Invited to save Greece from Macedonian control, Rome entered the eastern arena only to emerge by 146 as the ruler of Macedon and much of Greece. The great Seleucid Empire also fell to the Romans, and the weak Ptolemies of Egypt quickly made alliances with the colossus on the Tiber. By the middle of the first century B.C. Rome was the most powerful state in the ancient world.

Well aware of the novel grandeur of their growing empire, most Romans attributed their dominion to divine will. Tibullus' phrase, *Roma aeterna*, is characteristic of their hope for the future. With prophetic fervor, Vergil caused Jupiter to announce that to the Romans

"I have set no limits in space or time; they shall rule forever." The historian Livy, reflecting the views of his patron Augustus, depicts Rome as divinely sponsored. Any act against Rome was impiety, for the Romans were a chosen people. Even after the Empire had waned and had become Christian, St. Augustine of Hippo concluded that the pagan Romans had attained world dominion through God's favor. Since the Romans were virtuous, he argued, God had rewarded them with victory, though not with heaven. Such ascriptions of Rome's rise to divine grace scarcely constitute serious historical answers to the problem, but are contemporary views which in modern terms amount to a conviction that the rise of Rome cannot be explained in rational terms. On the other hand, Plutarch, who was not a Roman but a native of Greece and a priest of Delphi, offers a less pious answer than Livy and St. Augustine in suggesting that Tyche, "Lady Luck," was responsible for Rome's dominion.

Not all ancient writers were content to explain Rome's success as simple good fortune or divine favor. The historian Polybius saw the Achaean League, in which he was deeply involved, conquered by Rome. He maintains that the Republic's constitution unified the Romans behind their government, and that this solidarity of purpose enabled Rome to turn her city-state into a world empire. A modern circumstantial explanation for Rome's transformation from a city-state is given by the nineteenth-century scholar Numa-Denys Fustel de Coulanges. De Coulanges is concerned with the role of religion in the social and political life of the ancient world. Most ancient communities were exclusive; one had to be born into citizenship in order to worship, vote or hold office. In Rome, De Coulanges maintains, religious freedom led to an easy assimilation of many faiths and peoples, an amalgamation which conquered the world.

Ancient theorists blended geographic and racial factors to explain their empires. Aristotle attempted to prove Greek superiority over barbarians through ethnic geography, and the engineer Vitruvius Pollio applies a similar argument to Rome:

Though Southern peoples have sharper wits and fine strategy, they fail when courage is needed because the sun has sapped their strength. Those born in colder lands are more bravely braced for battle, but fail because they are slow of mind and plan poorly. . . . Those people balancing physical and mental strength precisely are the Italians. . . . And so Rome defeats the northern barbarians by her planning, the clever southerners by her strength. Thus Providence has given the Romans a fine temperate climate, so they can rule the world. (*De Architectura* VI.1.9–11)

The historian Max Cary provides a modern account of the significance of Mediterranean geography in the fourth selection, considering transportation routes as the key factor in Rome's growth. The noted economic historian Tenney Frank also discusses geography, arguing that failure of the soil and overpopulation forced the Romans to expand their territory in order to survive. Elsewhere, Professor Frank ascribes Rome's fall to racial mixture and implies that Rome's rise was due to the purity of her Italic stock, an argument he does not use here.[1]

One school of thought ascribes Rome's Empire to the character of her citizens. This argument is at least as old as Rome's national poet, Vergil, who declaims:

Others shall hammer soft the breathing bronze
And carve from marble faces true to life;
Shall eloquently plead, and know the paths
And tell the rising times of distant stars.
You Romans rule the peoples; know it well—

These are your arts: to keep the peace with law,
To spare the conquered and put down the proud!
(*Aeneid* VI, 847–853)

Many authors since have seen the Romans so, but few would wish to phrase the description so heroically. R. H. Barrow emphasizes the subordination of the Roman agrarian character to the gods, to elected officials and to a common purpose. Less complimentary to the Romans than Barrow, the Italian historian Guglielmo Ferrero views the Romans as a nation of conservative farmers who were mediocre in character. Ferrero, in his introduction to the American edition of *The Greatness and Decline of Rome*, suggests that: "An American easily understands the working of the old Roman state because he is a citizen of a state based on the same principle." Ferrero further explains that the Romans began their expansion with good intentions, but after they had conquered Carthage they lost their purity of character and became decadent. All the major powers were defeated, he finds, by well-meaning but mediocre Roman citizens.

Unlike other countries in other times, the Romans quite openly discussed their world empire and their right to rule. The orator Cicero explained Roman imperialism in the following terms:

For the Roman people to be slaves to others is wrong, since the immortal gods have willed us to rule all nations. . . . Other peoples can bear enslavement; the right of the Romans is liberty. (*Philippica* VI, vii, 19)

Writers since Cicero's time have discussed the extent to which Rome planned for and sought the Empire she eventually came to rule. In the tenth selection, Theodor Mommsen, the great German scholar of the last century, states that Rome's empire was forced upon her against her wish and without her connivance. Taking the opposite extreme, Stringfellow Barr finds in Rome's expansion the concerted employment of military force which was calculated to sub-

[1] "Race Mixture in the Roman Empire," *American Historical Review* XXI (1916), 689–708, reprinted in *Decline and Fall of the Roman Empire*, ed. Donald Kagan (Boston: D. C. Heath, 1962), 44–56.

ject the ancient world. Professor Barr finds in the emerging Roman Republic parallels with twentieth-century America, and is quite distressed by the apparent similarity between the two nations. "Let us assume that our swift, successful rise to world power confirms us, as a less swift rise once confirmed Rome, in believing that . . . the only sure tools for persuading are the stick and the carrot for donkeys, gunfire and money for men. . . .[2] The Baron de Montesquieu, on the other hand, sees the Romans as using any means to their end of power, but is apparently undismayed. Born to political power in eighteenth-century France, classically educated and widely traveled, Montesquieu writes with a cool clarity few others have ever attained. He weighed Platonic political theory (the most noble government will be the most successful) against Machiavellian principles (power is the end in itself), and found Machiavelli to be justified.

After reading this sample of views, the student will recognize that the puzzle of the rise of Rome can have no simple solution. As the French historian Leon Homo attempts to point out, no one cause can be found to account for such complex phenomena. Leon Homo's discussion of Roman imperialism is a synthesis of many opinions and forms a pleasant respite from the partisan accounts already read.

The puzzle of the rise of Rome involves the basic issue of historical causation. Any event in the past resulting from men's actions was affected by interacting personal and environmental factors about which historians can only speculate. Knowing this uncertainty, the scholar will hypothesize but will usually avoid dogmatism. A historian who proposes a simple solution to a major question is probably overlooking important data, while the careful scholar is content to advance one small piece in the puzzle and tentatively set it in place.

[2] *Consulting the Romans, An Occasional Paper on the Free Society* (Santa Barbara, California: Center for the Study of Democratic Institutions, 1967), 15.

CONFLICT OF OPINION

Therefore let us ascribe to none but the true God the power to grant kingdom and empire to men. And so the one true God . . . granted to the Romans an Empire when He willed it and as far-flung as He willed.

—AUGUSTINE

Yet clearly the smooth flow of events and the speed of Rome's rise to power and greatness shows that the spread of the Roman rule was not caused by the work of men, but was helped by the divine favoring wind of Lady Luck.

—PLUTARCH

Thus Rome was marked out by Nature to be the capital of a unified Italy, just as Italy, by virtue of its large man-power and relatively central situation within the Mediterranean lands, was the natural seat of a Mediterranean empire. Rome's lordship over the ancient Mediterranean world was in accordance with the basic facts of Mediterranean geography.

—M. CARY

The Roman population was, then, a mixture of several races, its worship was an assemblage of several worships, and its national hearth an association of several hearths. It was almost the only city whose municipal religion was not isolated from all others. It was related to all Italy and all Greece. There was hardly a people that it could not admit to its hearth.

—F. DE COULANGES

From the earliest days of Rome we can detect in the Roman a sense of dedication, at first crude and inarticulate and by no means unaccompanied by fear. In later days it is clearly expressed and is often a mainspring of action. . . . This is the clue to Roman character and to Roman history.

—R. H. BARROW

If we glance back at the career of Rome from the union of Italy to the dismemberment of Macedonia, the universal empire of Rome, far from appearing as a gigantic plan contrived and carried out by an insatiable thirst for territorial aggression, appears to have been a result which forced itself on the Roman government without, and even in opposition to, its wish.

—T. MOMMSEN

It was a slow way of conquering. They conquered a people and were content to weaken it. They imposed on it conditions which insensibly diminished it. If it rose up, they humbled it still further. Finally it became a subject without anyone being able to name the time of subjugation.

—MONTESQUIEU

I. PROVIDENTIAL FACTORS

Livy

PIETY AND THE BLESSING OF THE GODS

A noted writer in an age consciously trying to exalt the Roman Empire, Livy was commissioned to create a history of Rome which would emphasize the background of pious virtue of the Mediterranean's masters. Below is an excerpt from Livy's version of the speech which Camillus was said to have delivered to the Senate after the Gallic invasion of 390 B.C., when many favored abandoning the site of Rome for Veii. Obviously, this speech reflects the views of Livy's own time, especially in the reference to "empire." How far might confidence in divine favor help or hinder the growth of an empire?

WHY did we save Rome from the hands of our enemies, if we are to desert her now? When the victorious Gauls had the city in their power, the gods of Rome and the men of Rome still clung to the Capitol and the Citadel—and shall we now, in the hour of victory, voluntarily abandon even those strongholds which we held through the days of peril? Shall victory make Rome more desolate than defeat? Even were there no sacred cults coeval with Rome and handed down from generation to generation, so manifest at this time has been the power of God working for our deliverance that I, for one, cannot believe that any man could slack his duties of worship and thanksgiving. Only consider the course of our history during these latter years: you will find that when we followed God's guidance all was well; when we scorned it, all was ill. Remember the war with Veii—so long, so hard—and how it ended only when we obeyed the divine injunction and drained the Alban Lake. And what of this unprecedented calamity which has just befallen us? It never showed its ugly head till we disregarded the Voice from heaven warning us that the Gauls were coming— till our envoys violated the law of nations and we, who should have punished that crime, were again so careless of our duty to God as to let it pass. That is why we suffered defeat; that is why Rome was captured, and offered us again for gold; that is why we have been so punished by gods and men as to be an example to the world.

"Evil times came—and then we remembered our religion: we sought the protection of our gods on the Capitol, by the seat of Jupiter Greatest and Best; having lost all we possessed, we buried our holy things, or took them away to other towns, where no enemy would see them; though abandoned by gods and men, we never ceased to worship. Therefore it is that heaven has given us back our city and re-

From Livy, *The Early History of Rome,* translated by Aubrey de Selincourt (Harmondsworth, England: 1961), 381–82, 385–86. Reprinted by permission of Penguin Books Ltd.

stored to us victory and the old martial glory we had forfeited, turning the horror of defeat and death upon the enemy who, in his blind avarice for more gold, was disloyal to his compact and his plighted word. As you consider these manifest instances of the effect upon human destiny of obedience or of disobedience to the divine, can you not understand the heinousness of the sin which, though we have barely as yet won to shore from the shipwreck brought on us by our former guilt, we are preparing to commit? We have a city founded with all due rites of auspice and augury; not a stone of her streets but is permeated by our sense of the divine; for our annual sacrifices not the days only are fixed, but the places too, where they may be performed: men of Rome, would you desert your gods—the tutelary spirits which guard your families, and those the nation prays to as its saviours? Would you leave them all?

*   *   *

"Not without reason did gods and men choose this spot for the site of our City—the salubrious hills, the river to bring us produce from the inland regions and sea-borne commerce from abroad, the sea itself, near enough for convenience yet not so near as to bring danger from foreign fleets, our situation in the very heart of Italy—all these advantages make it of all places in the world the best for a city destined to grow great. The proof is the actual greatness—now—of a city which is still comparatively young; Rome, my friends, is 365 years old, and throughout those years you have been at war with many ancient peoples, yet—not to speak of single enemies—not the united strength of the powerful townships of the Aequians and Volscians, not the combined might of the armies and navies of Etruria, whose vast domains occupy the breadth of Italy from sea to sea, has ever been a match for you in war. What then in the devil's name makes you want to try elsewhere, when such has been your fortune here? Should you go, I grant you may take your brave hearts with you, but never the Luck of Rome. Here is the Capitol, where, in the days of old, the human head was found and men were told that on that spot would be the world's head and the seat of empire; here, when the Capitol was to be cleared of other shrines for the sake of Jupiter's temple, the two deities Juventas and Terminus refused, to the great joy of the men of those days, to be moved; here are the fires of Vesta, the sacred shields which fell from heaven, and all our gods who, if you stay, will assuredly bless your staying."

Camillus's oration is said to have moved his hearers, especially those parts of it which touched upon religion, but it was not decisive; what finally settled the matter was the chance remark of a centurion on duty. Soon after Camillus had ended, the Senate was holding a debate in the Curia Hostilia, and some soldiers returning from guard-duty happened to pass through the Forum; as they reached the Comitium, their centurion gave the order to halt, adding, "we might as well stop here." The words were heard in the Senate House; the senators hurried out exclaiming that they accepted the omen, and the crowd in the street signified its approval. The proposal for the migration was rejected, and the rebuilding of the city began.

St. Augustine of Hippo

WHY GOD CHOSE ROME

Living in the evening of the Roman Empire, St. Augustine of Hippo (354–430 A.D.) wrote *The City of God* to answer pagan attacks upon Christianity after Alaric sacked Rome in 410. Augustine's theory of history is that the pagan gods offer no help for man since the only source of divine aid is the Christian God, and that whatever success the Romans achieved was owed not to their ancestral pantheon but to the God of the Christians.

LET us see then what element in the Roman character moved the true God to think fit to aid the increase of the Roman Empire; for in His power are all earthly empires. . . . Roman history tells us, inviting our approval, that the early Romans (in spite of worshipping false gods and sacrificing victims to daemons, as did all nations except the Jews, instead of to God) were "greedy of praise, generous in money-dealings, ambitious in pursuit of world-wide glory and of riches honourably acquired." Glory was their supreme passion; for this they wished to live, for this they did not hesitate to die. All other desires they curbed in order to give rein to this absorbing ambition. In short, they thought it inglorious to be a subject people and glorious to rule and to be an imperial power; and so they ardently desired their country, first, to be free and then to rule an empire; and to these ends they devoted all their effort. . . .

The famous Oriental empires had long been in existence when God willed that a Western empire should come into being which should be later in time but before all others in the glory of its wide dominions and its greatness. To subdue the evils which oppressed the many nations He chose to grant the empire to men of such quality as were the Romans. For the sake of honour and praise and glory the Romans subordinated everything to their country's good, demanding that in their country they should receive that glory; and they did not hesitate to prefer their country's welfare to their own, curbing desire for money and many other vices to satisfy that one vice of which we have spoken, namely love of praise. . . .

The great men of Roman history were citizens of an earthly city. In all their devotion to that city they set before themselves the aim of promoting her safety. Their kingdom was not in Heaven but on earth, not in the life eternal but in the departure of dying men and the replacement of them by men soon to die. What else could they have loved except glory? By means of

Reprinted by permission of Faber and Faber Ltd. from *Introduction to St. Augustine*, translated by R. H. Barrow (London, 1950), 48–58. The footnotes in this edition have been omitted.

glory they wished to enjoy even after death a kind of a life in the praises of posterity.

To men of this kind God was not likely to grant eternal life in company with His holy angels in His heavenly city. Entry to that fellowship is given only by true religion which renders service and worship (called by the Greeks λατρεία) only to the one true God. If however He had not granted to them the earthly glory of a splendid empire (as He did), they would not receive, you might argue, the just reward for their good qualities, the virtues by which they strove to attain to such glory. Now in reply to those who are seen to do good that they may win glory from men the Lord says, "Verily I say unto you they have reaped their reward." This was true of the Romans; in the interest of the common weal, that is of the commonwealth and its treasury, they disregarded their own wealth, they resisted avarice, they promoted the prosperity of their country by a policy of freedom, they yielded neither to sin, as defined by their laws, nor to selfish desires. They relied upon these qualities to lead them as by a veritable high road to honour, empire and glory. And they did obtain their glory in almost all nations; upon many nations they imposed the laws of their empire, and to-day their glory is written in the literature and history of most nations. They have no reason to complain of the righteous justice of the all-high and true God: they have reaped their reward.

Very different is the reward of the saints who even here endure insult for the sake of the truth of God, which is hated by those who love this world.

The city of God endures for ever; in it no-one is born because no-one dies, in it dwells true and plentiful happiness—happiness which is not regarded as a goddess (as among the Romans) but as the gift of God. From this city we have received a pledge of faith as long as we sojourn here and sigh after its beauty; in it the sun does not rise upon the good and the evil, but the sun of righteousness shines only upon the good; in it there will be no anxious effort to enrich the public treasury by restricting private wealth, for there the treasure is shared by all alike and it is the treasure of the truth. Wherefore there were two reasons why the Roman empire was expanded and won glory from men; first, that due reward might be given to its citizens who were of the character which I have described, secondly, that the citizens of the eternal city during their sojourn here might study with sober diligence the examples set before them in Roman history, and might perceive how much affection they owe to their heavenly country in order to win eternal life, if the earthly city has inspired such affection in its own citizens that they may win glory among men.

You might ask what difference it makes under whose government a man lives—for his life lasts but a few days and then ceases and he is destined to die—provided that those who govern him do not compel him to acts of impiety or unrighteousness. But the Romans did no harm to the nations whom they conquered and brought under their own laws, except that they did these things at the cost of tremendous slaughter in wars. If only they could have imposed their laws by agreement, they would have brought about the same result more successfully (though then they would not have enjoyed the glory of triumph); and indeed they themselves actually lived under the laws which they imposed on the rest of the world. If this could have been done without invoking Mars and Bellona and without giving Victory a place in the picture (for there must be battles if there is to be a victor), then without doubt the Romans would have been on one and the same plane with the rest of the world. Particularly would this have been true if that most acceptable and equitable measure had been brought in earlier than in fact it was—I mean the extension of the fellowship of the state to all belonging to the Roman Empire so that they became Roman citizens and the privileges of the few were granted to all alike. But even so the landless populace would have depended for a livelihood on public funds; it would have been more acceptable, surely, if under a system of good state administration the means of that livelihood had been provided by agreement rather than extorted from defeated peoples. . . .

I have explained to the best of my ability the reason why the one true and righteous God aided the Romans, who were good if judged by the rough standards of the earthly city, to attain the glory of so great an empire. All the same there may be another reason which does not lie so much on the surface, since the varied merits which are to be found in the human race are known to God rather than to us. To all who are truly religious it is obvious that true religion—the true worship of the true God—is essential to true virtue, which cannot be true if it is directed towards worldly reputation. Yet they would hold that men who were not citizens of the everlasting city (called in our sacred literature the city of God) are of greater service to the earthly state if they have virtue as a possession without true religion than if they have no virtue at all. If however under the inspiration of true religion men lead good lives and possess also the skill to rule peoples, there can be no greater fortune for humanity than that under the mercy of God power should be in their hands. Such men attribute their high qualities, such as they can be in this life, to no source but the grace of God, knowing that He has given them in response to their wish, their belief and their prayer. At the same time they are aware how great are their short-comings in comparison with the perfection of the righteousness which is to be found in the fellowship of the holy angels, for which they strive to fit themselves. However much praise and credit may be given to the virtue which unaccompanied by true religion aims at worldly reputation, it is certainly not to be compared even with the earliest and slenderest efforts of the saints, whose hope is set·in the grace and mercy of the true God.

Therefore let us ascribe to none but the true God the power to grant kingdom and empire to men. God gives only to those who worship Him happiness in the kingdom of Heaven. Earthly kingdom He gives alike to those who do and to those who do not, according to His will who wills nothing unjust. I have stated a truth which He willed should be clear to us. None the less it is beyond me and it defeats the powers of us men to disclose what is hidden and to pass clear and transparent judgement upon the merits of this or that kingdom. And so the one true God who did not leave the human race without His guidance and help granted to the Romans an Empire when He willed it and as far-flung as He willed.

Plutarch

THE LUCK OF THE ROMANS

Plutarch of Chaeronea (c. 46–120 A.D.) produced an immense amount of material divided into two main bodies, the *Moralia* (moral essays) and the *Parallel Lives*. Widely traveled, he had been to Rome, had taught philosophy there, and had acquired influential Roman friends. "The Luck of the Romans," from which this selection is drawn, is a debate between the Goddesses of Luck and Virtue, each contending for the credit of Rome's dominion. We have only the first part, Lady Luck's argument; Virtue's argument is apparently lost. It is quite obvious that Plutarch's version of Roman history is as much fancy as fact, a compound of myth and reality which no modern scholar would term history. Yet, in terms of modern historical scholarship, Plutarch seems to urge consideration of the *casual* reasons for Rome's emergence, without denying the existence of *causal* factors also. Is the casual factor a valid historical interpretation of cause? How far should such an explanation be carried?

VIRTUE and Lady Luck have had many great debates, and are now beginning the greatest of all: which of them deserves the credit for the foundation and the rise of the mighty Roman Empire. The winner of the debate will receive not merely praise but also a defense against common criticism. For Virtue is called beautiful but unprofitable, and Lady Luck undependable, though good. They say Virtue's works are useless and Luck's gifts are untrustworthy. But if the Roman Empire is credited to the work of either Goddess, who can say that Virtue is useless if she has done so much good for good men, or that Luck is fickle if she has stayed behind the Romans so long? . . . .

Now I think that although Virtue and Lady Luck have been in constant and violent conflict, yet they apparently made a truce to raise the powerful Empire, this loveliest of human works. . . .

With no one supreme ruler over all, while everyone wanted to dominate, the world was full of unspeakable violence, confusion and instability. Then Rome rose to its full strength, took under its power not only neighboring peoples but also those far across the seas, and laid the foundation of firmness and stability needed for the Empire to make a circle of peace. Virtue of all kinds was in those who managed this, but great Luck was also present, as will be apparent from what follows here. . . .

Lady Luck approaches this debate swiftly, boldly, and most optimistically. She runs far ahead of Virtue. . . . After deserting the Persians and Assyrians, flying lightly over

From Plutarchus, *Plutarchi Moralia*, edited by W. Nachstadt, W. Sieveking & J. B. Titchener (Lipsiae: B. G. Teubner, 1935), v. 2, fasc. 2, pp. 43–49, 51–54, 56–62, 66–68. Translated by the editor rendering Tyche as "Lady Luck."

Macedonia and quickly shaking off Alexander, making her way through Egypt and Syria and then supporting the Carthaginians, she has crossed the Tiber to the Palatine, and apparently given up her wings, sandals and unsteady globe. So she entered Rome, showing she meant to stay, and so she is here at her trial today. . . .

Let us now call in the Romans as witnesses for Lady Luck, since they attributed their success more to Luck than to Virtue. . . . At least, it was only recently, after many years, that the Romans have built shrines to Virtue, Honor and Reason. . . . Even today they have no shrine for Wisdom or Prudence or Generosity or Faithfulness or Moderation. But for Lady Luck there are splendid ancient shrines dating back almost to the foundation of the City. The first to build a Temple to Luck was Ancus Marcius, the fourth king of Rome and the grandson of Numa. Her Temple was also built in the gardens Caesar bequeathed to the people, since they believed that even he reached eminence through good Luck, as he himself said.

If Julius Caesar had not stated himself that he reached eminence by good luck, I would hesitate to say this. When on a January fourth he set out from Brundisium after Pompey, he crossed the sea safely though it was the time for the winter solstice, because Lady Luck postponed the season. When he found Pompey overwhelmingly entrenched on land with a large fleet at sea, while his own troops were small in number since his reinforcements had not yet arrived, Caesar dared to disguise himself as a servant and slip away on a small boat, unrecognized by the captain and the pilot. But when the pilot was about to turn back because the river current was too rough against the tidal surge, Caesar pulled his cloak back from his head to reveal himself and said, "Go on, sir, fear nothing! Trust your sails to Lady Luck and you will bear her winds. Have courage, for you bear Caesar and Caesar's Luck with you." He was that firmly convinced that Lady Luck was with him on his voyages and journeys, his campaigns and armies. It was up to her to make the sea calm, bring summer weather in winter, hasten the slowest men, and encourage the most discouraged. More unbelievable than all this, it was Lady Luck that made Pompey flee and Ptolemy murder this guest, so Pompey fell and yet Caesar escaped the guilt of killing him. . . .

But we must also introduce the testimony of historical events dating back to the beginning of Rome. In the first place, who would deny that Luck laid the foundations in the birth, preservation, care and development of Romulus, and that Virtue finished the building? It does seem that the circumstances of the origin and birth of Rome's founders and builders were marvelously lucky. Their mother is said to have slept with a god, and the records say that the sun was eclipsed by the moon, making a long night, when the god Mars mated with the human Sylvia. And the same thing, they say, happened when Romulus died: he disappeared during an eclipse of the sun. . . .

Later, when the twins were born and a tyrant gave orders to do away with them, Lady Luck arranged that no barbarous or savage servant took them, but a kind man who did not kill them. The servant put the babies by the edge of a river near a green meadow in the shade of bushes. . . . Then a she-wolf that had lost her cubs, her teats swollen and overflowing with milk so she badly needed relief, circled around the babies and let them suck. Also a woodpecker, sacred to Mars, came and perched near, opening the mouth of each child in turn with a claw and placing inside a bite of its own food. . . .

Surely the fact that they were not discovered while they were raised and educated in Gabii, so no one knew they were the sons of Sylvia and the grandsons of King Numitor, seems to be a clever secret scheme of Luck. They escaped dying for their royal lineage before doing their work, but their noble birth could be recognized later as their successes made their nobility obvious. . . .

This, I think, is what Lady Luck says to Romulus' Virtue: "Your deeds are brilliant and mighty, and you have truly proved yourself divine in blood and birth. But do you see how far behind me you are? If I had not been at his birth to help him, if I had deserted the babies, how could you have come to such shining splendor? If then instead of the she-wolf needing to feed some creature from her overflowing teats, some completely savage, hungry beast had come, these lovely palaces, theaters, promenades, forums and public buildings would be herdsmen's huts and shepherds' fields, subject to some lord of Alba or Etruria or Latium." Everyone knows that the beginning is always the most important, especially in founding and building a city. Luck

provided this beginning by saving and guarding Rome's founder. Virtue made Romulus great, but Luck watched over him until he became great. . . .

Lady Luck took charge of the city when it was threatened by the wars of neighboring tribes and by internal struggles as if by a storm at sea, and calmed the jealous passions as if they were gusts of wind. They say that when young kingfishers go to sea in winter storms, the sea keeps them safe and cares for them. Just so Luck brought a calm over the affairs of Rome, keeping the city isolated from war or plague or danger or panic. So the newly settled and threatened people had a chance to establish their city so it might grow securely, in quiet. A freighter or trireme is built by violent blows of hammers and nails, bolts and saws and axes, but when it is finished it must rest for a while until its fastenings have firmed together; if it is launched while its joints are still damp and slippery, the waves will loosen them and let in the sea. Just so Romulus, the first ruler, took on a heavy load in organizing the city from farmers and shepherds, and faced wars and many dangers to defeat those who opposed the founding of Rome.

But Numa, the second ruler, had the Luck to consolidate and ensure the expansion of Rome in peace and quiet. If then some Porsenna had advanced and set up an Etruscan camp and stockade beside the new, unstable walls, or if some Marsian rebel chief had arrived ready for war, or some jealous Lucanian warmonger like Mutilus or Silo or Sulla's last opponent, Telesinus—any of these would have overwhelmed Numa, the pious lover of wisdom. The early city could not have resisted and grown to such a strong population.

As it is, probably the peace of Numa's time prepared the people for later wars. Like an athlete, the city trained quietly during the forty-three years after Romulus and grew strong enough to cope with their later enemies in war. They say that no famine or plague or crop failure or other disaster disturbed Rome in those years, as if it were not human wisdom but Lady Luck herself in charge of Rome in those crucial years. All that time the double door of Janus' temple, which the Romans call the gates of War, was shut; for it is open when there is war and closed when peace is made.

But after Numa died this door was opened, since war had begun with the Albans. Then many other wars followed without a pause until the door was closed in the peace after the Punic Wars, 480 years later. After a year it was opened again, and wars continued until Augustus' victory at Actium. Then the Roman armies rested, but not for long. The troubles with the Cantabrians and the Gauls, and at the same time with the Germans, interrupted the peace. These things are recorded here as evidence of Numa's great good Luck. . . .

However, so we will not seem to avoid the brighter evidence by retreating into the dim past, let us now leave the kings and discuss the most famous deeds and wars. Who would not admit that much daring courage was needed in these wars?. . . . Yet clearly the smooth flow of events and the speed of Rome's rise to power and greatness shows that the spread of the Roman rule was not caused by the work of men, but was helped by the divine favoring wind of Lady Luck.

Trophy is set on trophy, triumph follows triumph, and blood still warm on their swords is washed away by more. They counted their victories not by the number of corpses and spoils, but by kingdoms captured, nations enslaved, and islands and continents added to their empire. In one battle Philip lost Macedonia; at one stroke Antiochus was beaten back from Asia; in one defeat the Carthaginians lost Africa.

Pompey alone in one swift campaign added Armenia, Pontus, the Euxine, Syria, Arabia, Albania, Iberia, and all the territory as far as the Caucasus and the Hyrcanians to Rome. Three times his victories reached the Ocean that surrounds the inhabited world, because in Africa he drove the Numidians back to the shores of the Southern Sea; he subdued Spain, which had favored the rebel Sertorius, as far as the Atlantic; he chased the Albanian Kings until he stopped them near the Caspian Sea. All his successes were due to the Luck of the Romans. Then at last he met his own fate.

The Luck of the Romans sent a favorable wind, not too briefly at its best like the Macedonian, not only a land breeze like the Athenian, nor late to rise like the Persian, nor quick to stop like the Carthaginian. This Luck from the first grew in maturity, strength, and wisdom together with the City, and was faithful to it on land and sea, in war and peace, against foreigners and Greeks.

II. FAVORABLE CIRCUMSTANCES

Polybius

CONSTITUTIONAL STRENGTH

A Greek hostage taken to Italy after Rome conquered Macedon in 168, Polybius (c. 204–122 B.C.) became friendly with such influential Romans as the consuls Aemilius Paulus and Scipio Aemilianus. Polybius had been present at the siege of Carthage in the Third Punic War, advising his friends. His resulting familiarity with these two major powers led him to contrast Rome's political strength with weaknesses he found inherent in Carthage's more democratic constitution. He was thus able to study Rome's strength without denigrating his own conquered homeland in comparison. Can a historian today assert that a nation with an aristocratic constitution is more apt to conquer?

I AM aware that some will be at a loss to account for my interrupting the course of my narrative for the sake of entering upon the following disquisition on the Roman constitution. But I think that I have already in many passages made it fully evident that this particular branch of my work was one of the necessities imposed on me by the nature of my original design; and I pointed this out with special clearness in the preface which explained the scope of my history. I there stated that the feature of my work which was at once the best in itself, and the most instructive to the students of it, was that it would enable them to know and fully realise in what manner, and under what kind of constitution, it came about that nearly the whole world fell under the power of Rome in somewhat less than fifty-three years,—an event certainly without precedent. This being my settled purpose, I could see no more fitting period than the present for making a pause, and examining the truth of the remarks about to be made on this constitution. In private life if you wish to satisfy yourself as to the badness or goodness of particular persons, you would not, if you wish to get a genuine test, examine their conduct at a time of uneventful repose, but in the hour of brilliant success or conspicuous reverse. For the true test of a perfect man is the power of bearing with spirit and dignity violent changes of fortune. An examination of a constitution should be conducted in the same way: and therefore being unable to find in our day a more rapid or more signal change than that which has happened to Rome, I reserved my disquisition on its constitution for this place. . . .

What is really educational and beneficial to students of history is the clear view of the causes of events,

From *The Histories of Polybius,* translated by Evelyn Shuckburgh (London, 1889), 458–459, 467–474, 501–506. Footnotes in this and subsequent selections have been omitted.

and the consequent power of choosing the better policy in a particular case. Now in every practical undertaking by a state we must regard as the most powerful agent for success or failure the form of its constitution; for from this as from a fountainhead all conceptions and plans of action not only proceed, but attain their consummation.

* * *

I am fully conscious that to those who actually live under this constitution I shall appear to give an inadequate account of it by the omission of certain details. Knowing accurately every portion of it from personal experience, and from having been bred up in its customs and laws from childhood, they will not be struck so much by the accuracy of the description, as annoyed by its omissions; nor will they believe that the historian has purposely omitted unimportant distinctions, but will attribute his silence upon the origin of existing institutions or other important facts to ignorance. What is told they depreciate as insignificant or beside the purpose; what is omitted they desiderate as vital to the question: their object being to appear to know more than the writers. But a good critic should not judge a writer by what he leaves unsaid, but from what he says: if he detects mis-statement in the latter, he may then feel certain that ignorance accounts for the former; but if what he says is accurate, his omissions ought to be attributed to deliberate judgment and not to ignorance. So much for those whose criticisms are prompted by

personal ambition rather than by justice. . . .

Another requisite for obtaining a judicious approval for an historical disquisition, is that it should be germane to the matter in hand; if this is not observed, though its style may be excellent and its matter irreproachable, it will seem out of place, and disgust rather than please. . . .

As for the Roman constitution, it had three elements, each of them possessing sovereign powers: and their respective share of power in the whole state had been regulated with such a scrupulous regard to equality and equilibrium, that no one could say for certain, not even a native, whether the constitution as a whole were an aristocracy or democracy or despotism. And no wonder: for if we confine our observation to the power of the Consuls we should be inclined to regard it as despotic; if on that of the Senate, as aristocratic; and if finally one looks at the power possessed by the people it would seem a clear case of a democracy. What the exact powers of these several parts were, and still, with slight modifications, are, I will now state.

The Consuls, before leading out the legions, remain in Rome and are supreme masters of the administration. All other magistrates, except the Tribunes, are under them and take their orders. They introduce foreign ambassadors to the Senate; bring matters requiring deliberation before it; and see to the execution of its decrees. If, again, there are any matters of state which require the authorization of the people, it is their business to see to them, to summon the popular meetings, to bring the proposals before them, and to carry out the decrees of the majority. In the preparations for war also, and in a word in the entire administration of a campaign, they have all but absolute power. It is competent to them to impose on the allies such levies as they think good, to appoint the Military Tribunes, to make up the roll for soldiers and select those that are suitable. Besides they have absolute power of inflicting punishment on all who are under their command while on active service: and they have authority to expend as much of the public money as they choose, being accompanied by a quaestor who is entirely at their orders. A survey of these powers would in fact justify our describing the constitution as despotic,—a clear case of royal government. Nor will it affect the truth of my description, if any of the institutions I have described are changed in our time, or in that of our posterity: and the same remarks apply to what follows.

The Senate has first of all the control of the treasury, and regulates the receipts and disbursements alike. For the Quaestors cannot issue any public money for the various departments of the state without a decree of the Senate, except for the service of the Consuls. The Senate controls also what is by far the largest and most important expenditure, that, namely, which is made by the censors every *lustrum* [a period of five years] for the repair or construction of public buildings; this money cannot be obtained by the censors except by the grant of the Senate. Similarly all crimes committed in Italy requiring a public investigation, such as treason, conspiracy, poisoning, or wilful murder, are in the hands of the Senate. Besides, if any individual or state among the Italian allies requires a controversy to be settled, a penalty to be assessed, help or protection to be afforded,—all this is the province of the Senate. Or again, outside Italy, if it is necessary to send an embassy to reconcile warring communities, or to remind them of their duty, or sometimes to impose requisitions upon them, or to receive their submission, or finally to proclaim war against them,—this too is the business of the Senate. In like manner the reception to be given to foreign ambassadors in Rome, and the answers to be returned to them, are decided by the Senate. With such business the people have nothing to do. Consequently, if one were staying at Rome when the Consuls were not in town, one would imagine the constitution to be a complete aristocracy: and this has been the idea entertained by many Greeks, and by many kings as well, from the fact that nearly all the business they had with Rome was settled by the Senate.

After this one would naturally be inclined to ask what part is left for the people in the constitution, when the Senate has these various functions, especially the control of the receipts and expenditure of the exchequer; and when the Consuls, again, have absolute power over the details of military preparation, and an absolute authority in the field? There is, however, a part left the people, and it is a most important one. For the people is the sole fountain of honour and of punishment; and it is by these two things and these alone that dynasties and constitutions and, in a word, human society are held together: for where the distinction between them is not sharply drawn both in theory and practice, there no undertaking can be properly administered,—as indeed we might expect when good and bad are held in exactly the same honour. The people then are the only court to decide matters of life and death; and even in cases where the penalty is money, if the sum to be assessed is sufficiently serious, and especially when the accused have held the higher magistracies. And in regard to this arrangement there is one point deserving especial commendation and record. Men who are on trial for their lives at Rome, while sentence is in process of being voted,—if even only one of the tribes whose votes are needed to ratify the sentence has not voted,—have the privilege at Rome of openly departing and condemning themselves to a voluntary exile. Such men are safe at Naples or Praeneste or at Tibur, and at other towns with which this arrangement has been duly ratified on oath.

Again, it is the people who bestow offices on the deserving, which are the most honourable rewards of virtue. It has also the absolute power of passing or repealing laws; and, most important of all, it is the people who deliberate on the question of peace or war. And when provisional terms are made for alliance, suspension of hostilities, or treaties, it is the people who ratify them or the reverse.

These considerations again would lead one to say that the chief power in the state was the people's, and that the constitution was a democracy.

Such, then, is the distribution of power between the several parts of the state. I must now show how each of these several parts can, when they choose, oppose or support each other.

The Consul, then, when he has started on an expedition with the powers I have described, is to all appearance absolute in the administration of the business in hand; still he has need of the support both of people and Senate, and, without them, is quite unable to bring the matter to a successful conclusion. For it is plain that he must have supplies sent to his legions from time to time; but without a decree of the Senate they can be supplied neither with corn, nor clothes, nor pay, so that all the plans of a commander must be futile, if the Senate is resolved either to shrink from danger or hamper his plans. And again, whether a Consul shall bring any undertaking to a conclusion or no depends entirely upon the Senate: for it has absolute authority at the end of a year to send another Consul to supersede him, or to continue the existing one in his command. Again, even to the successes of the generals the Senate has the power to add distinction and glory, and on the other hand to obscure their merits and lower their credit. For these high achievements are brought in tangible form before the eyes of the citizens by what are called "triumphs." But these triumphs the commanders cannot celebrate with proper pomp, or in some cases celebrate at all, unless the Senate concurs and grants the necessary money. As for the people, the Consuls are pre-eminently obliged to court their favour, however distant from home may be the field of their operations; for it is the people, as I have said before, that ratifies, or refuses to ratify, terms of peace and treaties; but most of all because when laying down their office they have to give an account of their administration before it. Therefore in no case is it safe for the Consuls to neglect either the Senate or the goodwill of the people.

As for the Senate, which possesses the immense power I have described, in the first place it is obliged in public affairs to take the multitude into account, and respect the wishes of the people; and it cannot put into execution the penalty for offences against the republic, which are punishable with death, unless the people first ratify its decrees. Similarly even in matters which directly affect the senators,—for instance, in the case of a law diminishing the Senate's traditional authority, or depriving senators of certain dignities and offices, or even actually cutting down their property,—even in such cases the people have the sole power of passing or rejecting the law. But most important of all is the fact that, if the Tribunes interpose their veto, the Senate not only are unable to pass a decree, but cannot even hold a meeting at all, whether formal or informal. Now, the Tribunes are always bound to carry out the decree of the people, and above all things to have regard to their wishes: therefore, for all these reasons the Senate stands in awe of the multitude, and cannot neglect the feelings of the people.

In like manner the people on its part is far from being independent of the Senate, and is bound to take its wishes into account both collectively and individually. For contracts, too numerous to count, are given out by the censors in all parts of Italy for the repairs or construction of public buildings; there is also the collection of revenue from many rivers, harbours, gardens, mines, and land—everything, in a word, that comes under the control of the Roman government: and in all these the people at large are engaged; so that there is scarcely a man, so to speak, who is not interested either as a contractor or as being employed in the works. For some purchase the contracts from the censors for themselves; and others go partners with them; while others again go security for these contractors, or actually pledge their property to the treasury for them. Now over all these transactions the Senate has absolute control. It can grant an extension of time; and in case of unforeseen accident can relieve the contractors from a portion of their obligation, or release them from it altogether, if they are absolutely unable to fulfil it. And there are many details in which the Senate can inflict great hardships, or, on the other hand, grant great indulgences to the contractors: for in every case the appeal is to it. But the most important point of all is that the judges are taken from its members in the majority of trials, whether public or private, in which the charges are heavy. Consequently, all citizens are much at its mercy; and bring alarmed at the uncertainty as to when they may need its aid, are cautious about resisting or actively opposing its will. And for a similar reason men do not rashly resist the wishes of the Consuls, because one and all may become subject to their absolute authority on a campaign.

The result of this power of the several estates for mutual help or harm is a union sufficiently firm for all emergencies, and a constitution than which it is impossible to find a better. For whenever any danger from without compels them to unite and work together, the strength which is developed by the State is so extraordinary, that everything required is unfailingly carried out by the eager rivalry shown by all classes to devote their whole minds to the need of the hour, and to secure that any determination come to should not fail for want of promptitude; while each individual works, privately and publicly alike, for the accomplishment of the business in hand. Accordingly, the peculiar constitution of the State makes it irresistible, and certain of obtaining whatever it determines to attempt. Nay, even when these external alarms are past, and the people are enjoying their good fortune and the fruits of their victories, and, as usually happens, growing corrupted by flattery and idleness, show a tendency to violence and arrogance,—it is in these circumstances, more than ever, that the constitution is seen to possess within itself the power of correcting abuses. For when any one of the three classes becomes puffed up, and manifests an inclination to be contentious and unduly encroaching, the mutual interdependency of all the three, and the possibility of the pretensions of any one being checked and thwarted by the others, must plainly check this tendency: and so the proper equilibrium is maintained by the impulsiveness of the one part being checked by its fear of the other.

* * *

Now the Carthaginian constitution seems to me originally to have been well contrived in these most distinctively important particulars. For they had kings, and the Gerusia had the powers of an aristocracy, and the multitude were supreme in such things as affected them; and on the whole the adjustment of its several parts was very like that of Rome and Sparta. But about the period of its entering on the Hannibalian war the political state of Carthage was on the decline, that of Rome improving. For whereas there is in every body, or polity, or business a natural stage of growth, zenith, and decay; and whereas everything in them is at its best at the zenith; we may thereby judge of the difference between these two constitutions as they existed at that period. For exactly so far as the strength and prosperity of Carthage preceded that of Rome in point of time, by so much was Carthage then past its prime, while Rome was exactly at its zenith, as far as its political constitution was concerned. In Carthage therefore the influence of the people in the policy of the state had already risen to be supreme, while at Rome the Senate was at the height of its power: and so, as in the one measures were deliberated upon by the many, in the other by the best men, the policy of the Romans in all public undertakings proved the stronger; on which account, though they met with capital disasters, by force of prudent counsels they finally conquered the Carthaginians in the war.

If we look however at separate details, for instance at the provisions for carrying on a war, we shall find that whereas for a naval expedition the Carthaginians are the better trained and prepared,—as it is only natural with a people with whom it has been hereditary for many generations to practise this craft, and to follow the seaman's trade above all nations in the world,—yet, in regard to military service on land, the Romans train themselves to a much higher pitch than the Carthaginians. The former bestow their whole attention upon this department: whereas the Carthaginians wholly neglect their infantry, though they do take some slight interest in the cavalry. The reason of this is that they employ foreign mercenaries, the Romans native and citizen levies. It is in this point that the latter polity is preferable to the former. They have their hopes of freedom ever resting on the courage of mercenary troops: the Romans on the valour of their own citizens and the aid of their allies. The result is that even if the Romans have suffered a defeat at first, they renew the war with undiminished forces, which the Carthaginians cannot do. For, as the Romans are fighting for country and children, it is impossible for them to relax the fury of their struggle; but they persist with obstinate resolution until they have overcome their enemies. What has happened in regard to their navy is an instance in point. In skill the Romans are much behind the Carthaginians, as I have already said; yet the upshot of the whole naval war has been a decided triumph for the Romans, owing to the valour of their men. For although nautical science contributes largely to success in sea-fights, still it is the courage of the marines that turns the scale most decisively in favour of victory. The fact is that Italians as a nation are by nature superior to Phoenicians and Libyans both in physical strength and courage; but still their habits also do much to inspire the youth with enthusiasm for such exploits. One example will be sufficient of the pains taken by the Roman state to turn out men ready to endure anything to win a reputation in their country for valour.

Whenever one of their illustrious men dies, in the course of his funeral, the body with all its paraphernalia is carried into the forum to the Rostra, as a raised platform there is called, and sometimes is propped upright upon it so as to be conspicuous, or, more rarely, is laid upon it. Then with all the people standing round, his son, if he has left one of full age and he is there, or, failing him, one of his relations, mounts the Rostra and delivers a speech concerning the virtues of the deceased, and the successful exploits performed by him in his lifetime. By these means the people are reminded of what has been done, and made to see it with their own eyes,—not only such as were engaged in the actual transactions but those also who were not;—and their sympathies are so deeply moved, that the loss appears not to be confined to the actual mourners, but to be a public one affecting the whole people. After the burial and all the usual ceremonies have been performed, they place the likeness of the deceased in the most conspicuous spot in his house, surmounted by a wooden canopy or shrine. This likeness consists of a mask made to represent the deceased with extraordinary fidelity both in shape and colour. These likenesses they display at public sacrifices adorned with much care. And when any illustrious member of the family dies, they carry these masks to the funeral, putting them on men whom they thought as like the originals as possible in height and other personal peculiarities. And these substitutes assume clothes according to the rank of the person represented: if he was a consul or praetor, a toga with purple stripes; if a censor, whole purple; if he had also celebrated a triumph or performed any exploit of that kind, a toga embroidered with gold. These representatives also ride themselves in chariots, while the fasces and axes, and all the other customary insignia of the particular offices, lead the way, according to the dignity of the rank in the state enjoyed by the deceased in his lifetime; and on arriving at the Rostra they all take their seats on ivory chairs in their order. There could not easily be a more inspiring spectacle than this for a young man of noble ambitions and virtuous aspirations. For can we conceive any one to be unmoved at the sight of all the likenesses collected together of the men who have earned glory, all as it were living and breathing? Or what could be a more glorious spectacle?

Besides the speaker over the body about to be buried, after having finished the panegyric of this particular person, starts upon the others whose representatives are present, beginning with the most ancient, and recounts the successes and achievements of each. By this means the glorious memory of brave men is continually renewed; the fame of those who have performed any noble deed is never allowed to die; and the renown of those who have done good service to their country becomes a matter of common knowledge to the multitude, and part of the heritage of posterity. But the chief benefit of the ceremony is that it inspires young men to shrink from no exertion for the general welfare, in the hope of obtaining the glory which awaits the brave. And what I say is confirmed by this fact. Many Romans have volunteered to decide a whole battle by single combat; not a few have deliberately accepted certain death, some in time of war to secure the safety of the rest, some in time of peace to preserve the safety of the commonwealth. There have also been instances of men in office putting their own sons to death, in defiance of every custom and law, because they rated the interests of their country higher than those of natural ties even with their nearest and dearest. There are many stories of this kind, related of many men in Roman history; but one will be enough for our present purpose; and I will give the name as an instance to prove the truth of my words.

The story goes that Horatius Cocles, while fighting with two enemies at the head of the bridge over the Tiber, which is the entrance to the city on the north, seeing a large body of men advancing to support his enemies, and fearing that they would force their way into the city, turned round, and shouted to those behind him to hasten back to the other side and break down the bridge. They obeyed him: and whilst they were breaking the bridge, he remained at his post receiving numerous wounds, and checked the progress of the enemy: his opponents being panic stricken, not so much by his strength as by the audacity with which he held his ground. When the bridge had been broken down, the attack of the enemy was stopped; and Cocles then threw himself into the river with his armour on and deliberately sacrificed his life, because he valued the safety of his country and his own future reputation more highly than his present life, and the years of existence that remained to him. Such is the enthusiasm and emulation for noble deeds that are engendered among the Romans by their customs.

Again the Roman customs and principles regarding money transactions are better than those of the Carthaginians. In the view of the latter nothing is disgraceful that makes for gain; with the former nothing is more disgraceful than to receive bribes and to make profit by improper means. For they regard wealth obtained from unlawful transactions to be as much a subject of reproach, as a fair profit from the most unquestioned source is of commendation. A proof of the fact is this.

The Carthaginians obtain office by open bribery, but among the Romans the penalty for it is death. With such a radical difference, therefore, between the rewards offered to virtue among the two peoples, it is natural that the ways adopted for obtaining them should be different also.

But the most important difference for the better which the Roman commonwealth appears to me to display is in their religious beliefs. For I conceive that what in other nations is looked upon as a reproach, I mean a scrupulous fear of the gods, is the very thing which keeps the Roman commonwealth together. To such an extraordinary height is this carried among them, both in private and public business, that nothing could exceed it. Many people might think this unaccountable; but in my opinion their object is to use it as a check upon the common people. If it were possible to form a state wholly of philosophers, such a custom would perhaps be unnecessary. But seeing that every multitude is fickle, and full of lawless desires, unreasoning anger, and violent passion, the only resource is to keep them in check by mysterious terrors and scenic effects of this sort. Wherefore, to my mind, the ancients were not acting without purpose or at random, when they brought in among the vulgar those opinions about the gods, and the belief in the punishments in Hades: much rather do I think that men nowadays are acting rashly and foolishly in rejecting them. This is the reason why, apart from anything else, Greek statesmen, if entrusted with a single talent, though protected by ten checking-clerks, as many seals, and twice as many witnesses, yet cannot be induced to keep faith: whereas among the Romans, in their magistracies and embassies, men have the handling of a great amount of money, and yet from pure respect to their oath ˙keep their faith intact. And, again, in other nations it is a rare thing to find a man who keeps his hands out of the public purse, and is entirely pure in such matters: but among the Romans it is a rare thing to detect a man in the act of committing such a crime.

Numa-Denys Füstel de Coulanges

THE MELTING POT

Füstel de Coulanges (1830–1889) taught "scientific history" at both Strasburg and Paris. His six volume *Histoire des institutions politiques de l'ancienne France* describes the origins of medieval France; *The Ancient City* analyzes the role religion played in the cities of antiquity. Written in 1864 before archaeology had its full impact on ancient history, *The Ancient City* may err in specifics but its thesis still merits consideration. Both Coulanges and Polybius discuss political institutions: Polybius emphasizes the Roman constitution while Coulanges stresses Roman subjects and allies. How do their views differ? Coulanges espouses a theory concerning the "melting pot" of antiquity quite parallel to Horace Kallen's "melting pot" theory of American history. Is this an adequate explanation for either American or Roman expansion?

AT first it appears very surprising that among the thousand cities of Greece and Italy one was found capable of subduing all the others. Yet this great event is due to the ordinary causes that determine the course of human affairs. The wisdom of Rome consisted, like all wisdom, in profiting by the favorable circumstance that fell in its way.

We can distinguish two periods in the work of the Roman conquest. One corresponds to the time when the old municipal spirit was still strong; it was then that Rome had the greatest number of obstacles to surmount. The second belonged to the time when the municipal spirit was much weakened; conquest then became easy, and was accomplished rapidly.

The origin of Rome and the composition of its people are worthy of remark. They explain the particular character of its policy, and the exceptional part that fell to it from the beginning in the midst of other cities.

The Roman race was strangely mixed. The principal element was Latin, and originally from Alba; but these Albans themselves, according to traditions which no criticism authorizes us to reject, were composed of two associated, but not confounded, populations. One was the aboriginal race, real Latins. The other was of foreign origin, and was said to have come from Troy with Æneas, the priest-founder; it was, to all appearance, not numerous, but was influential from the worship and the institutions which it had brought with it.

These Albans, a mixture of two races, founded Rome on a spot where another city had already been built—

From Füstel de Coulanges, *The Ancient City*, translated by Willard Small (Garden City, N.Y., n.d.), 360–367, 374–388.

Pallantium, founded by the Greeks. Now, the population of Pallantium remained in the new city, and the rites of the Greek worship were preserved there. There was also, where the Capitol afterwards stood, a city which was said to have been founded by Hercules, the families of which remained distinct from the rest of the Roman population during the entire continuance of the republic.

Thus at Rome all races were associated and mingled; there were Latins, Trojans, and Greeks; there were, a little later, Sabines, and Etruscans. Of the several hills, the Palatine was the Latin city, after having been the city of Evander. The Capitoline, after having been the dwelling-place of the companions of Hercules, became the home of the Sabines of Tatius. The Quirinal received its name from the Sabine Quirites, or from the Sabine god Quirinus. The Cœlian hill appears to have been inhabited from the beginning by Etruscans. Rome did not seem to be a single city; it appeared like a confederation of several cities, each one of which was attached by its origin to another confederation. It was the centre where the Latins, Etruscans, Sabellians, and Greeks met.

Its first king was a Latin; the second, a Sabine; the fifth was, we are told, the son of a Greek; the sixth was an Etruscan.

Its language was composed of the most diverse elements. The Latin predominated, but Sabellian roots were numerous, and more Greek radicals were found in it than in any other of the dialects of Central Italy. As to its name, no one knew to what language that belonged. According to some, Rome was a Trojan word; according to others, a Greek word. There are reasons for believing it to be Latin, but some of the ancients thought it to be Etruscan.

The names of Roman families also attest a great diversity of origin. In the time of Augustus there were still some fifty families who, by ascending the series of their ancestors, arrived at the companions of Æneas. Others claimed to be descendants of the Arcadian Evander, and from time immemorial the men of these families wore upon their shoes, as a distinctive sign, a small silver crescent. The Potitian and Pinarian families were descended from those who were called the companions of Hercules, and their descent was proved by the hereditary worship of that god. The Tullii, Quinctii, and Servilii came from Alba after the conquest of that city. Many families joined to their name a surname which recalled their foreign origin. There were thus the Sulpicii Camerini, the Cominii Arunci, the Sicinii Sabini, the Claudii Regillenses, and the Aquillii Tusci. The Nautian family was Trojan, the Aurellii were Sabines; the Cæcilii came from Præneste, and the Octavii were originally from Velitræ.

The effect of this mixing of the most diverse nations was, that from the beginning Rome was related to all the peoples that it knew. It could call itself Latin with the Latins, Sabine with the Sabines, Etruscan with the Etruscans, and Greek with the Greeks.

Its national worship was also an assemblage of several quite different worships, each one of which attached it to one of these nations. It had the Greek worship of Evander and Hercules, and boasted of possessing the Trojan Palladium. Its Penates were in the Latin city of Lavinium, and it adopted from the beginning the Sabine worship of the god Consus. Another Sabine god, Quirinus, was so firmly established at Rome that he was associated with Romulus, its founder. It had also the gods of the Etruscans, and their festivals, and their augurs, and even their sacerdotal insignia.

At a time when no one had the right to take part in the religious festivals of a nation unless he belonged by birth to that nation, the Roman had this incomparable advantage of being able to take part in the Latin holidays, the Sabine festivals, the Etruscan festivals, and the Olympic games. Now, religion was a powerful bond. When two cities had a single worship, they called themselves relations; they were required to regard themselves as allies, and to aid each other. In ancient times men knew of no other union than that which religion established. Rome therefore preserved with great care whatever could serve as an evidence of this precious relationship with other nations. To the Latins it presented its traditions of Romulus; to the Sabines its legend of Tarpeia and Tatius; to the Greeks it quoted the old hymns which it had preserved in honor of Evander's mother, hymns which Romans no longer understood, but which they persisted in singing. They also preserved the recollection of Æneas with the greatest care; for if they could claim relationship with the Peloponnesians through Evander,

they were related through Æneas to more than thirty cities, scattered through Italy, Sicily, Greece, Thrace, and Asia Minor, all having had Æneas for a founder, or being colonies of cities founded by him,—all having, consequently, a common worship with Rome. We can see in the wars which they waged in Sicily against Carthage, and in Greece against Philip, what advantage they derived from this ancient relationship.

The Roman population was, then, a mixture of several races, its worship was an assemblage of several worships, and its national hearth an association of several hearths. It was almost the only city whose municipal religion was not isolated from all others. It was related to all Italy and all Greece. There was hardly a people that it could not admit to its hearth.

During the period when the municipal religion was everywhere powerful, it governed the policy of Rome.

We are told that the first act of the new city was to seize some Sabine women—a legend which appears very improbable when we reflect on the sanctity of marriage among the ancients; but we have seen above that the municipal religion forbade marriage between persons of different cities unless these two cities had a common origin or a common worship. The first Romans had the right of intermarriage with Alba, from which they originally came, but not with their other neighbors, the Sabines. What Romulus wished to obtain first of all was not a few women; it was the right of intermarriage,—that is to say, the right of contracting regular relations with the Sabine population. For this purpose a religious bond must be established between them; he therefore adopted the worship of the Sabine god Consus, and celebrated his festival. Tradition adds that during this festival he carried off the women. If he had done this, the marriages could not have been celebrated according to the rites, since the first and most necessary act of the marriage was the *traditio in manum,* —that is to say, the giving away of the daughter by the father; Romulus would have failed of his object. But the presence of the Sabines and their families at the religious ceremony, and their participation in the sacrifice, established between the two nations a bond such that the *connubium* could no longer be refused. There was no need of a seizure; the right of intermarriage was a natural consequence of the festival. And the historian Dionysius, who consulted ancient documents and hymns, assures us that the Sabines were married according to the most solemn rites, which is confirmed by Plutarch and Cicero. It is worthy of remark that the result of the first effort of the Romans was to throw down the barriers which the municipal religion had placed between two neighboring nations. No similar legend relative to Etruria has come down to us, but it appears quite certain that Rome had the same relations with that country as with Latium and the Sabines. The Romans therefore had the address to unite themelves, by worship and by blood, with all the nations around them. They took care to have the *connubium* with all the cities; and what proves that they

well understood the importance of this bond is, that they would not permit other cities, their subjects, to have it among themselves.

Rome then entered upon the long series of its wars. The first was against the Sabines of Tatius; it was terminated by a religious and political alliance between these two little nations. It next made war upon Alba. The historians say that the Romans dared to attack this city, though they were a colony from it. It was precisely because they were a colony from Alba that they judged it necessary to destroy that city. Indeed, every metropolis exercised a religious supremacy over its colonies, and religion then had so great an influence that while Alba remained standing, Rome could be only a dependent city, and her progress would be forever arrested.

After the destruction of Alba, Rome was no longer content to remain a colony, but claimed to take the rank of a metropolis, by inheriting the rights and the religious supremacy which up to that time Alba had exercised over the thirty colonies of Latium. The Romans sustained long wars to obtain the presidency of the sacrifice at the *feriœ Latinœ* [Latin festivals]. This was a means of acquiring the single kind of superiority and dominion which was understood at that time.

They built at home a temple to Diana; they obliged the Latins to come and offer sacrifices there, and even attracted the Sabines to it. By this means they habituated these two nations to share with them, under their presidency, the festivals, the prayers, and the sacred flesh of the victims. Rome thus united them under her religious supremacy.

Rome was the only city that understood how to augment her population by war. The Romans pursued a policy unknown to the rest of the Græco-Italian world; they annexed all that they conquered. They brought home the inhabitants of captured cities, and gradually made Romans of them. At the same time they sent colonists into the conquered countries, and in this manner spread Rome everywhere; for their colonists, while forming distinct cities, in a political point of view, preserved a religious community with the metropolis; and this was enough to compel the colonies to subordinate their policy to that of Rome, to obey her, and to aid her in all her wars.

One of the remarkable peculiarities of the policy of Rome was, that she attracted to her all the worships of the neighboring cities. She obtained possession of a Juno from Veii, a Jupiter from Præneste, a Minerva from Falerii, a Juno from Lanuvium, a Venus from the Samnites, and many others that we do not know. "For it was the custom of the Romans," says one of the ancients, "to take home the religions of the conquered cities; sometimes they distributed them among the gentes, and sometimes they gave them a place in their national religion." Montesquieu praises the Romans for a refinement of skillful policy in not having imposed their gods upon the conquered nations. But that would have been contrary to their ideas, and to those of all the ancients Rome conquered

the gods of the vanquished, and did not give them hers. She kept her protectors for herself, and even labored to increase the number. She tried to possess more worships and more tutelary gods than any other city.

As, moreover, these worships and gods were, for the most part, taken from the conquered, Rome was placed by them in religious communion with all the surrounding nations. The ties of a common origin, the possession of the *connubium*, that of the presidency of the *feriæ Latinæ*, that of the vanquished gods, the right, which they pretended to have, of sacrificing at Olympia and at Delphi, were so many means by which the Romans prepared their dominion. Like all the cities, Rome had her municipal religion, the source of her patriotism; but she was the only city which made this religion serve for her aggrandizement. Whilst other cities were isolated by their religion, Rome had the address or the good fortune to employ hers to draw everything to herself, and to dominate over all.

* * *

The institutions of the ancient city had been weakened, and almost exhausted, by a series of revolutions. One of the first results of the Roman dominion was to complete their destruction, and to efface what still remained of them. This we can see by observing the condition into which the nations fell as they became subject to Rome.

We must first banish from our minds all the customs of modern politics, and not picture to ourselves the nations entering the Roman state, one after another, as in our day provinces are annexed to a kingdom, which, on receiving these new members, extends its boundaries. The Roman state (*civitas Romana*) was not enlarged by conquests; it never included any families except those that figured in the religious ceremony of the census. The Roman territory (*ager Romanus*) never increased. It remained enclosed within the immutable limits which the kings had traced for it, and which the ceremony of the *ambarvalia* [a boundary festival], sanctified every year. What increased with every conquest was the dominion of Rome (*imperium Romanum*).

So long as the republic lasted, it never entered the mind of any one that the Romans and the other peoples could form a single nation. Rome might, indeed, receive a few of the conquered, allow them to live within her walls, and transform them, in the course of time, into Romans; but she could not assimilate a whole foreign people to her people, an entire territory to her territory. Still this was not peculiar to the policy of Rome, but a principle that held through all antiquity; it was a principle from which Rome would sooner have departed than any other city, but from which she could not entirely free herself. Whenever, therefore, a people was conquered, it did not enter the Roman state; it entered only the Roman dominion. It was not united to Rome, as provinces are to-day united to a capital; between other nations and itself Rome knew only two kinds of connection—subjection or alliance.

From this it would seem that municipal institutions must have subsisted among the conquered, and that the world must have been an assemblage of cities distinct from each other, and having at their head a ruling city. But it was nothing of the kind. The effect of the Roman conquest was to work in every city a complete transformation.

On one side were the subjects *deditii*, or those who, having pronounced the formula of the *deditio* [capitulation], had delivered to the Roman people "their persons, their walls, their lands, their waters, their houses, their temples, and their gods."

They had therefore renounced, not only their municipal government, but all that appertained to it among the ancients,—that is to say, their religion and their private law. From that moment these men no longer formed a political body among themselves; nothing that goes to make up a regular society remained to them. Their city (*urbs*) might remain standing, but the state (*civitas*) had perished. If they continued to live together, they lived without institutions, laws, or magistrates. The arbitrary authority of a *præfectus* sent by Rome maintained material order among them. On the other hand were the allies—*fœderati*, or *socii*. They were less cruelly treated. The day on which they entered the Roman dominion, it had been stipulated that they should preserve their municipal government, and should remain organized into cities. They therefore continued to have in every city a constitution, magistracies, a senate, a prytaneum, laws, and judges. The city was supposed to be independent, and seemed to have no other relations with Rome than those of an ally with its ally. Still, in the terms of the treaty which had been drawn up at the time of the conquest, Rome had been careful to insert these words: *Majestatem populi Romani comiter conservato.* [They shall willingly uphold the dignity of the Roman people]. These terms established the dependence of the allied city upon the metropolitan city, and as they were very vague, it happened that the measure of this dependence was always in accordance with the will of the stronger. These cities, which were called free, received orders from Rome, obeyed proconsuls, and paid taxes to the collectors of the revenue. Their magistrates rendered their accounts to the governor of the province, who also heard the appeals from the judges. Now, such was the nature of the municipal system among the ancients that it needed complete independence, or it ceased to exist. Between the maintenance of the institutions of the city and their subordination to a foreign power, there was a contradiction which perhaps does not clearly appear to the eyes of the moderns, but which must have struck every man of that period. Municipal liberty and the government of Rome were irreconcilable; the first could be only an appearance, a falsehood, an amusement calculated to divert the minds of men. Each of those cities sent, almost every year, a deputation to Rome, and its most minute and most private affairs were regulated by the senate. They still had their municipal magistrates, their archons, and their strategi, freely elected by themselves; but the archon

no longer had any other duty than to inscribe his name on the registers for the purpose of marking the year, and the strategus, in earlier times the chief of the army and of the state, now had no other care than to keep the streets in order, and inspect the markets.

Municipal institutions, therefore, perished among the nations that were called allies as well as among those that bore the name of subjects; there was only this difference, that the first preserved the exterior forms. Indeed, the city, as antiquity had understood it, was no longer seen anywhere, except within the walls of Rome.

Then, too, the Romans, while everywhere destroying the municipal system, substituted nothing in its place. To the people whose institutions they took away, they did not give their own instead. The Romans never thought of creating new institutions for their use; they never made a constitution for the people of their empire, and did not understand how to establish fixed rules for their government. Even the authority which Rome exercised over the cities had no regularity. As they made no part of her state, or of her city, she had no legal power over them. Her subjects were strangers to her—a reason why she exercised this irregular and unlimited power which ancient municipal law allowed citizens to exercise towards foreigners and enemies. It was on this principle that the Roman administration was a long time regulated, and this is the manner in which it was carried on.

Rome sent one of her citizens into a country. She made that country the *province* of this man,—that is to say, his charge, his own care, his personal affair; this was the sense of the word *provincia*. At the same time she conferred upon this citizen the *imperium*; this signified that she gave up in his favor, for a determined time, the sovereignty which she held over the country. From that time this citizen represented in his person all the rights of the republic, and by this means he was an absolute master. He fixed the amount of taxes; he exercised the military power, and administered justice. His relations with the subjects, or the allies, were limited by no constitution. When he sat in his judgment-seat, he pronounced decisions according to his own will; no law controlled him, neither the provincial laws, as he was a Roman, nor the Roman laws, as he passed judgment upon provincials. If there were laws between him and those that he governed, he had to make them himself, for he alone could bind himself. Therefore the *imperium* with which he was clothed included the legislative power; and thus it happened that the governors had the right, and established the custom, on entering the provinces, of publishing a code of laws, which they called their Edict, and to which they morally promised to conform. But as the governors were changed annually, these codes changed every year, for the reason that the law had its source only in the will of the man who was for the time invested with the *imperium*. This principle was so rigorously applied that, when a judgment had been pronounced by a governor, but had not been entirely executed at the time of his departure from the province, the arrival of his successor completely an-

nulled this judgment, and the proceedings were recommenced.

Such was the omnipotence of the governor. He was the living law. As to invoking the justice of Rome against his acts of violence or his crimes, the provincials could not do this unless they could find a Roman citizen who would act as their patron, for, as to themselves, they had no right to demand the protection of the laws of the city, or to appeal to its courts. They were foreigners; the judicial and official language called them *peregrini* [aliens]; all that the law said of the *hostis* [enemy] continued to be applied to them.

The legal situation of the inhabitants of the empire appears clearly in the writings of the Roman jurisconsults. We there see that the people are considered as no longer having their own laws, and as not yet having those of Rome. For them, therefore, the law did not exist in any manner. In the eyes of the Roman jurisconsult, a provincial was neither husband nor father,—that is to say, the law recognized neither his marital nor his paternal authority. For him property did not exist. It was a double impossibility for him to become a proprietor; it was impossible by reason of his personal condition, because he was not a Roman citizen, and impossible by reason of the condition of the land, because it was not Roman territory, and the law admitted the complete right of ownership only within the limits of the *ager Romanus*. For the lawyers taught that the land in the provinces was never private property, and that men could have only the possession and usufruct thereof. Now, what they said in the second century of our era of the provincial territory had been equally true of the Italian soil before Italy obtained the Roman franchise, as we shall presently see.

It is certain, then, that the people, as fast as they entered the Roman empire, lost their municipal religion, their government, and their private law. We can easily believe that Rome softened in practice whatever was destructive in this subjection. We see, indeed, that, though the Roman laws did not recognize the paternal authority in the subject, they allowed this authority still to subsist in practice. If they did not permit a certain man to call himself a proprietor of the soil, they still allowed him the possession of it; he cultivated his land, sold it, and devised it by will. It was not said that this land was his, but they said it was as good as his, *pro suo*. It was not his property, *dominium*, but it was among his goods, *in bonis*. Rome thus invented for the benefit of the subject a multitude of turns and artifices of language. Indeed, the Roman genius, if its municipal traditions prevented it from making laws for the conquered, could not suffer society to fall into dissolution. In principle the provincials were placed outside the laws, while in fact they lived as if they had them; but with the exception of this, and the tolerance of the conquerors, all the institutions of the vanquished and all their laws were allowed to disappear. The Roman empire presented, for several generations, this singular spectacle: A single city remained intact, preserving its institutions and its laws, while all the rest—that is to say, more than a hundred millions of souls —either had no kind of laws, or had such as were not recognized by the ruling city. The world then was not precisely in a state of chaos, but force, arbitrary rule, and convention, in default of laws and principles, alone sustained society.

Such was the effect of the Roman conquest on the nations that successively became its prey. Of the city everything went to ruin; religion first, then the government, and finally private law. All the municipal institutions, already for a long time shaken, were finally overthrown and destroyed; but no regular society, no system of government, replaced at once what had disappeared. There was a period of stagnation between the moment when men saw the municipal governments dissolve and that in which another form of society appeared. The nation did not at once succeed the city, for the Roman empire in no wise resembled a nation. It was a confused multitude, where there was real order only in one central point, and where all the rest enjoyed only a factitious and transitory order, and obtained this only at the price of obedience. The conquered nations succeeded in establishing themselves as an organized body only by conquering in their turn the rights and institutions which Rome was inclined to keep for itself. In order to do this they had to enter the Roman city, make a place for themselves there, press forward, and transform that city also, in order to make of themselves and Rome one body. This was a long and difficult task.

We have seen how deplorable was the condition of the Roman subject, and how the condition of the citizen was to be envied. Not vanity alone, but the most real and dearest interests had to suffer. Whoever was not a Roman citizen was not reputed to be either a husband or a father; legally he could be neither proprietor nor heir. Such was the value of the title of Roman citizen, that without it one was outside the law, and with it he entered regular society. It happened, therefore, that this title became the object of the most lively desires of men. The Latin, the Italian, the Greek, and, later, the Spaniard and the Gaul, aspired to be Roman citizens—the single means of having rights and of counting for something. All, one after another, nearly in the order in which they entered the Roman empire, labored to enter the Roman city, and, after long efforts, succeeded. This slow introduction into the Roman state is the last act in the long history of the social transformations of the ancients. To observe this great event in all its successive phases, we must examine its commencement, in the fourth century before our era.

Latium had been conquered; of the forty small peoples who inhabited it, Rome had exterminated half. She had despoiled some of their lands, and had left to others the title of allies. In B.C. 340 the latter perceived that the alliance was entirely to their detriment, that they were expected to obey in everything, and that they were required every year to lavish their blood and money for the sole benefit of Rome. They formed a coalition; their chief, Annius, thus stated their demands in the Roman senate: "Give us equality. Let us have the same laws; let us form but a single state—*una civitas;* let us have but a single name; let us all alike be called Romans." Annius thus announced, in the year 340, the desire which all the nations of the empire, one after another expressed, and which was to be completely realized only after five centuries and a half. Then such a thought was new and very unexpected; the Romans declared it monstrous and criminal. It was, indeed, contrary to the old religion and the old law of the cities. The consul, Manlius, replied, that if such a proposition should be accepted, he would slay with his own hand the first Latin who should come to take his seat in the senate; then, turning towards the altar, he called upon the god to witness, saying, "Thou hast heard, O Jupiter, the impious words that have come from this man's mouth. Canst thou tolerate, O Jupiter, that a foreigner should come to sit in thy sacred temple as a senator, as a consul?" Thus Manlius expressed the old sentiment of repulsion that separated the citizen from the foreigner. He was the organ of the ancient religious law, which prescribed that the foreigner should be detested by the men because he was cursed by the gods of the city. It appeared to him impossible that a Latin should be a senator because the place of meeting for the senate was a temple, and the Roman gods could not suffer the presence of a foreigner in their sanctuary.

War followed: the Latins, being conquered, surrendered,—that is to say, they gave up to the Romans their cities, their worships, their laws, and their lands. Their position was cruel. A consul said in the senate that, if they did not wish Rome to be surrounded by a vast desert, the fate of the Latins should be settled with some regard to clemency. Livy does not clearly explain what was done. If we are to trust him, the Latins obtained the right of Roman citizenship without including in the political privileges the right of suffrage, or in the civil the right of marriage. We may also note, that these new citizens were not counted in the census. It is clear that the senate deceived the Latins in giving them the name of Roman citizens. This title disguised a real subjection, since the men who bore it had the obligations of citizens without the rights. So true is this, that several Latin cities revolted, in order that this pretended citizenship might be withdrawn.

A century passed, and, without Livy's notice of the fact, we might easily discover that Rome had changed her policy. The condition of the Latins having the rights of citizens, without suffrage and without *connubium*, no longer existed. Rome had withdrawn from them the title of citizens, or, rather, had done away with this falsehood, and had decided to restore to the different cities their municipal governments, their laws, and their magistracies.

But by a skilful device Rome opened a door which, narrow as it was, permitted subjects to enter the Roman city. It granted to every Latin who had been a magistrate in his native city the right to become a Roman citizen at the expiration of his term of office. This time the gift of this right was complete and without reserve; suffrage, magistracies, census, marriage, private law, all were included. Rome resigned itself to share with the foreigner its religion, its government, and its laws; only its favors were individual, and were addressed not to entire cities, but to a few men in each of them. Rome admitted to her bosom only what was best, wealthiest, and most estimable in Latium.

This right of citizenship then became precious, first, because it was complete, and secondly, because it was a privilege. Through it a man figured in the comitia of the most powerful city of Italy; he might be consul and commander of the legions. There was also the means of satisfying more modest ambitions; thanks to this right, one might ally himself, by marriage, to a Roman family; or he might take up his abode at Rome, and become a proprietor there; or he might carry on trade in Rome, which had already become one of the first commercial towns in the world. One might enter the company of farmers of the revenue,—that is to say, take a part in the enormous profits which accrued from the collection of the revenue, or from speculations in the lands of the *ager publicus*. Wherever one lived he was effectually protected; he escaped the authority of the municipal magistrate, and was sheltered from the caprices of the Roman magistrates themselves. By being a citizen of Rome, a man gained honor, wealth, and security.

The Latins, therefore, became eager to obtain this title, and used all sorts of means to acquire it. One day, when Rome wished to appear a little severe, she found that twelve thousand of them had obtained it through fraud.

Ordinarily, Rome shut her eyes, knowing that by this means her population increased, and that the losses of war were thus repaired. But the Latin cities suffered; their richest inhabitants became Roman citizens, and Latium was impoverished. The taxes, from which the richest were exempt as Roman citizens, became more and more burdensome, and the contingent of soldiers that had to be furnished to Rome was every year more difficult to fill up. The larger the number of those who obtained the Roman franchise, the harder was the lot of those who had not that right. There came a time when the Latin cities demanded that this franchise should cease to be a privilege. The Italian cities, which, having been conquered two centuries before, were in nearly the same condition as those of Latium, and also saw their richest inhabitants abandon them to become Romans, demanded for themselves the Roman franchise. The fate of subjects and allies had become all the less supportable at this period, from the fact that the Roman democracy was then agitating the great question of the agrarian laws. Now, the principle of all these laws was, that neither subject nor ally could be an owner of the soil, except by a formal act of the city, and that the greater part of the Italian lands belonged to the republic. One party demanded, therefore, that these lands, which were nearly all occupied by Italians, should be taken back by the state, and distributed among the poor of Rome. Thus the Italians were menaced with general ruin. They felt keenly the need of civil rights, and they could only come into possession of these by becoming Roman citizens.

The war that followed was called the *social war;* the allies of Rome took up arms that they might no longer be allies, but might become Romans. Rome, though victorious, was still constrained to grant what was demanded, and the Italians received the rights of citizenship. Thenceforth assimilated to the Romans, they could vote in the forum; in private life they were governed by Roman laws; their right to the soil was recognized, and the Italian lands, as well as Roman soil, could be owned by them in fee simple. Then was established the *jus Italicum:* this was the law, not of the Italian person, since the Italian had become a Roman, but of the Italian soil, which was susceptible of ownership, just as if it had been the *ager Romanus.*

From that time all Italy formed a single state. There still remained the provinces to enter into the Roman unity.

We must make a distinction between Greece and the provinces of the west. In the west were Gaul and Spain, which, before the conquest, knew nothing of the real municipal system. The Romans attempted to create this form of government among them, either thinking it impossible to govern them otherwise, or judging that, in order gradually to assimilate them to the Italian nations, it would be necessary to make them pass over the same route which the Italians had followed. Hence it happened that the emperors who suppressed all political life at Rome, kept up the forms of municipal liberty in the provinces. Thus cities were formed in Gaul; each had its senate, its aristocratic body, its elective magistrates; each had even its local worship, its

Genius, and its city-protecting divinity, after the manner of those in ancient Greece and ancient Italy. Now, this municipal system, thus established, did not prevent men from arriving at the Roman citizenship; on the contrary, it prepared them for it. A gradation, skilfully arranged among these cities, marked the steps by which they were insensibly to approach Rome, and finally to become assimilated with it. There were distinguished, first, the allies, who had a government and laws of their own, and no legal bond with Roman citizens; second, the colonies, which enjoyed the civil rights of the Romans, without having political rights; third, the cities of the Italian right,—that is to say, those to whom, by the favor of Rome, the complete right of property over their lands had been granted, as if these lands had been in Italy; fourth, the cities of the Latin right, —that is to say, those whose inhabitants could, following the custom formerly established in Latium, become Roman citizens after having held a municipal office. These distinctions were so deep, that between persons of two different classes no marriage or other legal relation was possible. But the emperors took care that the cities should rise in the course of time, and one after another, from the condition of subjects or allies, to the Italian right, from the Italian right to the Latin right. When a city had arrived at this point, its principal families became Romans one after another.

Greece entered just as little into the Roman state. At first every city preserved the forms and machinery of the municipal government. At the moment of the conquest, Greece showed a desire to preserve its autonomy; and this was left to it longer, perhaps, than it would have wished. At the end of a few generations it aspired to become Roman; vanity, ambition, and interest worked for this.

The Greeks had not for Rome that hatred which is usually borne towards a foreign master. They admired it; they had a veneration for it; of their own accord they devoted a worship to it, and built temples to it as to a god. Every city forgot its protecting divinity, and worshipped in its place the goddess Rome and the god Cæsar; the greatest festivals were for them, and the first magistrates had no higher duty than celebrating with great pomp the Augustan games. Men thus became accustomed to lift their eyes above their cities; they saw in Rome the model city, the true country, the prytaneum of all nations. The city where one was born seemed small. Its interests no longer occupied their minds; the honors which it conferred no longer satisfied their ambition. Men thought themselves nothing if they were not Roman citizens. Under the emperors, it is true, this title no longer conferred political rights; but it offered more solid advantages, since the man who was clothed with it acquired at the same time the full right to hold property, the right to inherit, the right to marry, the paternal authority, and all the private rights of Rome. The laws which were found in each city were variable and without foundation; they were merely tolerated. The Romans despised them, and the Greeks had little respect for them. In order to have fixed laws, recognized by all as truly sacred, it was necessary to have those of Rome.

We do not see that all Greece, or even a Greek city, formally asked for this right of citizenship, so much desired; but men worked individually to acquire it, and Rome bestowed it with a good grace. Some obtained it through the favor of the emperor; others bought it. It was granted to those who had three children, or who served in certain divisions of the army. Sometimes to construct a merchant vessel of a certain tonnage, or to carry grain to Rome, was sufficient to obtain it. An easy and prompt means of acquiring it was to sell one's self as a slave to a Roman citizen, for the act of freeing him according to legal forms conferred the right of citizenship. One who had the title of Roman citizen no longer formed a part of his native city, either civilly or politically. He could continue to live there, but he was considered an alien; he was no longer subject to the laws of the city, he no longer obeyed its magistrates, no longer supported its pecuniary burdens. This was a consequence of the old principle, which did not permit a man to belong to two cities at the same time. It naturally happened that, after several generations, there were in every Greek city quite a large number of men, and these ordinarily the wealthiest, who recognized neither its government nor its laws. Thus slowly, and as if by a natural death, perished the municipal system. There came a time when the city was a mere framework that contained nothing, where the local laws applied to hardly a person, where the municipal judges no longer had anything to adjudicate upon.

Finally, when eight or ten generations had sighed for the Roman franchise, and all those who were of any account had obtained it, there appeared an imperial decree which granted it to all free men without distinction.

What is remarkable here is, that no one can tell the date of this decree or the name of the prince who issued it. The honor is given, with some probability of truth, to Caracalla,—that is to say, to a prince who never had very elevated views; and this is attributed to him as simply a fiscal measure. We meet in history with few more important decrees than this. It abolished the distinction which had existed since the Roman conquest between the dominant nation and the subject peoples; it even caused to disappear a much older distinction, which religion and law had made between cities. Still the historians of that time took no note of it, and all we know of it we glean from two vague passages of the jurisconsults and a short notice in Dion Cassius. If this decree did not strike contemporaries, and was not remarked by those who then wrote history, it is because the change of which it was the legal expression had been accomplished long before. The inequality between citizens and subjects had been lessened every generation, and had been gradually effaced. The decree might pass unperceived under the veil of a fiscal measure; it proclaimed and caused to pass into the domain of law what was already an accomplished fact.

The title of citizen then began to fall into desuetude; or, if it was still employed, it was to designate the condition of a free man as opposed to that of a slave. From that time all that made a part of the Roman empire, from Spain to the Euphrates, formed really one people and a single state. The distinction between cities had disappeared; that between nations still appeared, but was hardly noticed. All the inhabitants of this immense empire were equally Romans. The Gaul abandoned his name of Gaul, and eagerly assumed that of Roman; the Spaniard, the inhabitant of Thrace, or of Syria, did the same. There was now but a single name, a single country, a single government, a single code of laws.

We see how the Roman city developed from age to age. At first it contained only patricians and clients; afterwards the plebeian class obtained a place there; then came the Latins, then the Italians, and finally the provincials. The conquest had not suf-

ficed to work this great change; the slow transformation of ideas, the prudent but uninterrupted concessions of the emperors, and the eagerness of individual interests had been necessary. Then all the cities gradually disappeared, and the Roman city, the last one left, was itself so transformed that it became the union of a dozen great nations under a single master. Thus fell the municipal system.

It does not belong to our plan to tell by what system of government this was replaced, or to inquire if this change was at first more advantageous than unfortunate for the nations. We must stop at the moment when the old social forms which antiquity had established were forever effaced.

Max Cary

THE GEOGRAPHIC ADVANTAGE

The English historian Max Cary (1881–1958) co-edited *The Oxford Classical Dictionary* and contributed articles to *The Cambridge Ancient History*. Perhaps his year in Athens after his Oxford education led to his special interest in geographic factors in ancient history. Cary seems to hold that the Mediterranean is naturally suited to unification and that Rome's location was a primary factor in her dominance. What empires have existed since, and from what centers have they been controlled? To what extent does technology influence the geography of power?

THE pervasive influence of Mediterranean geography on the Greeks and Romans is illustrated in numerous features of their social and political life.

The Mediterranean climate makes for an open-air existence. Where summer heat is tempered by the play of breezes, and winter chill by a clear sun, life out of doors is pleasant over the greater part of the year. This open-air habit found expression in the plans of Greek and Roman houses, for those whose owners could afford the necessary ground space were usually laid out round one or more courts— a practice which survives in the less 'Europeanized' regions of the Mediterranean. In the cities shady recesses from the summer sun and the winter downpours are almost a necessity. The streets of Mediterranean towns have therefore from time immemorial been made as narrow as is consistent with traffic requirements, the side-alleys on hill sites often being mere staircases of the 'Clovelly' type; and the Greek and Roman architects who planned 'show' streets in the major cities made a point of lining them with porticoes and colonnades. In the streets and open squares of the towns rich and poor alike met their friends, spent their leisure, and transacted much of their business; and they sought their entertainment in unroofed theatres and arenas (the concert halls alone being covered over). For political affairs it was not only the massed Popular Assemblies that met in the open. The Areopagus at Athens held session in a porch (the *Stoa Basilike*), and the Dicasteries in open courts (in the literal sense); at Rome magistrates set up their tribunals in the Forum or one of its adjacent porticoes.

With these open-air habits went a readiness of social contacts and a general use of intercourse that made every Greek or Roman town into an informal club. Though aristocratic

From Max Cary, *The Geographic Background of Greek and Roman History* (Oxford, 1949), 31–36, 128–133, by permission of the Clarendon Press, Oxford.

personages might be accompanied on their outings by an escort of retainers, to save themselves from too intimate a contact with the common folk, they did not withdraw themselves from its gaze, but courted it in their public appearances. A similar tradition of affability, or at least of accessibility, was observed by political leaders; even kings and tyrants obeyed the law of *civilitas*, and it was not until the third century of the Christian era that Roman emperors accepted the Oriental custom of mysterious seclusion in the recesses of a palace.

[The density of settlement in Mediterranean lands is regulated to a large degree by one of their determinant features, the general scarcity of natural water-supplies in summer. The Anglo-Saxon 'tun,' with its population of one hundred persons or less, could not be reproduced here, except in the pockets of softer rock where the winter rains percolated more evenly through the subsoil, so as to provide an easily tapped store of water.] On the more usual limestone formations the irregular distribution of water necessitated a closer aggregation near the infrequent water-points —at a river-side or, more commonly, in the neighbourhood of a spring. Here substantial and closely built villages, with populations of 500 persons or over, would be formed, and under favourable conditions the villages would grow into towns with several thousand inhabitants. Though political and economic factors must also be invoked to explain the genesis and the siting of ancient Mediterranean cities, the primary factor of water-supply usually determined the growth of the villages which were the nuclei of the towns.

The habits of communal solidarity which life in compact settlements everywhere engenders were reinforced in Mediterranean lands by the need of joint action in the matter of water regulation—the provision of drainage canals for the winter floods and, more especially, the equitable rationing of supplies for irrigation.] To this extent life on the Mediterranean country-side provided a schooling for the more intensive co-operation of the members of a city-state.]

[But if natural conditions in Mediterranean lands made for communal co-operation, they did not favour agrarian communism. This form of organization is most compatible with a pastoral economy. But under Mediterranean conditions the prevailing type of land-work consisted of tillage and orchard cultivation. In these occupations, and especially in the tending of gardens, success must largely depend on the individual's devotion to his particular plot, and (in the absence of any highly organized machinery of state) this could be best assured by the institution of personal property.]

[Yet the natural economy of the Mediterranean lands did not play into the hands of capitalist exploitation. The generally broken and tumbled surface of the country did not favour the consolidation of plots into large units like the Bonanza farms of the American Middle West;] consequently the savings in production costs that result from operations on a big scale could not be realized, save in abnormal districts. Least of all could standardization and the processes of mass-production be introduced into the numerous corners and pockets where garden cultivation was practised, for here individual skill and attention prevailed over organization. The absorption of small property into the ownership of wealthy landlords, which was a recurrent feature of Greek and (more especially) of Roman history, was due in the main to political and social rather than to strictly economic causes. On the one hand, the exigencies of military service, which called the peasant away from his plot and might leave it untended for long periods, continual devastation by invaders (as in the later days of the Roman empire), and the lure of 'bread and circuses' in the cities, were so many inducements for the small owner to sell out; on the other hand, the social prestige and (in some states) the political privileges that accrued to landed property, and the general lack of other safe objects of investment, turned every moneyed person into an eager buyer. Even so, concentration of ownership did not necessarily entail the merging of small units of cultivation into *latifundia*. Having regard to the conditions imposed by Nature, some wealthy landlords made their purchases in small and scattered parcels, and those who consolidated their holdings into compact blocks not infrequently let them out in small lots, instead of applying organized methods of capitalist exploitation. The only branch of land work which gave any decisive advantage to operations on a large scale was 'transhumance' pasturing, for under proper organization hardly any more labour was required for the tending and droving of large herds than of small ones. Whatever the method of ownership, *la petite culture* remained the normal practice in ancient landwork.

[Another natural feature of the Mediterranean lands which left its mark on Greek and Roman history was the more or less abrupt transition from the cultivated lowlands to the maquis and the summer pasture of the upper zones, and the consequent segregation of the husbandman from the herdsman. From this dissociation natural enmities sprang up in the ancient world, such as still obtain between Fellahin and Bedouin in the Near East.] For the mobile and armed herdsman it was a constant temptation to supplement his scant living by raiding the plains, and to rid himself of this recurrent nuisance the lowlander had to organize his resources of greater man-power. The feud between Mountain and Plain runs like a red thread through early Roman history, culminating in the hard-fought and critical Samnite wars; and mindful of their early tradition as guardians of the Italian lowlands, the Romans subsequently pacified large tracts of provincial land by the drastic method of *deductio in plana* [removal down to the plains] of unruly upland populations. Yet the practice of 'transhumance', entailing a voluntary *deductio in plana* for herdsmen in the winter season, and a bargaining about the regular use of grazing-spaces in the lowlands, tended to overlay ancient feuds with emergent understandings, and the drovers' codes which Roman lawyers drew up for Italian pasturages confirmed the Roman soldiers' work of pacification. The need for highlanders to import salt for themselves and their herds also laid the foundations of friendly traffic between Mountain and Plain, and the Via Salaria, which led from the salt-pans of Ostia through Rome to the Sabine mountains, was as much a path of peace as an invasion track.

A more potent inducement to peace, however, was the intensive cultivation of olive and vine in Mediterranean lands. Tillers of the crop-land had periods of rest in their calendar, during which they could afford to take a holiday in the form of a campaign against some neighbouring state: even though the battle should go against them and their crops should suffer ravage, the damage was no greater than a year's hard work to follow could repair. But the labour in the vineyards was continuous, and the destruction of an olive-tree might require half a lifetime to make good. It was, therefore, no mere fancy which caused the Greeks and Romans to offer an olive branch as a symbol of peace.

But the most important natural factor in ancient Mediterranean history was the Mediterranean Sea itself. This great water has its dangerous moods, and throughout the ages it has scared some of its border peoples into remaining land-lubbers. But those who have adventured it and mastered its comparatively simple rules of navigation have earned their due reward in economic prosperity or political lordship. The fundamental similarity of the Mediterranean lands has not precluded disparities of detail between them sufficient to render them economically complementary to each other, and so to draw them together into habits of economic co-operation. Some regions were natural granaries, others were ill suited to corn-production but well adapted to produce wine or oil; and the raw materials of industry were variously distributed over the whole area. Thus the inter-Mediterranean traffic in foodstuffs and textiles, in ceramics and metal-ware, grew to be of basic importance for the material civilization of Greece and Rome; but the mass-movement of staple commodities would have been impossible without the commodious highway of the Mediterranean Sea.

This sea was equally indispensable as a connecting link between the members of any comprehensive political union. The importance of naval power in the Mediterranean as an instrument of empire may be illustrated from each successive thalassocracy of ancient times, from the Minoan, the Athenian, the Ptolemaic, and the Roman lordship of the seas. The part played by road communications in holding the Roman empire together should not be overlooked, but it was, above all, the Mediterranean Sea that enabled it to coalesce into an organic unity, for it alone could render possible that frequency of intercourse among its constituent parts which made them 'members of one another'. Seconded by wise Roman statesmanship, the natural uniting force of the Mediterranean Sea allowed the scattered populations of its borderland to achieve a cultural *bloc* which has ever since been a major factor in world civilization.

* * *

Occupying the central part of western Italy from the mouth of the Tiber to that of the Liris, Latium was described by Strabo as 'entirely fortunate and productive of all plants, except for a few marshy and unhealthy places along the coast and such parts as are mountainous and rocky'. This picture was too flattering, for the mountainous and rocky section extends over a considerable part of central and southern Latium, and the seaboard is not only swampy but devoid of good harbours. As a result, perhaps, of a subsidence in the sixth or fifth century B.C., the coast hardly rises above sea-level, and although some attempts were made in ancient times to improve its drainage—the canal from Rome to Terracina may have been intended for this purpose as well as for transport—the Pomptine marshes along it have retained their bad reputation until recently.

But Latium also possessed tracts which merited Strabo's encomium. At its south-eastern end the valley of the Liris broadened into a fertile alluvial basin; at the north-western edge of the mountains and in the valleys of the lower Tiber and Anio, the volcanic dust poured forth in prehistoric times from the Alban Mount formed a rich topsoil. This friable upper layer, it is true, needed protection against winter wash-outs; but a system of *cuniculi* [drainage canals]—perhaps a legacy from the Etruscan occupation—provided the

necessary drainage. The tall-grown forests of Latium which evoked the admiration of Theophrastus probably did not survive him for long; but the vineyards of its volcanic zone, which gained a high reputation under the early Roman emperors, were a lasting token of its productiveness. Latium as a whole was therefore able to subsist a relatively large population.

Apart from Fregellae in the Liris valley and Rome at the other extremity, the principal towns of Latium were situated at the north-western edge of the upland zone on spurs of high ground overlooking the Roman plain. Such were Tibur (Tivoli), girt by a loop of the Anio; Praeneste, which stood commandingly on a ledge of 1,350 feet and was in turn dominated by a citadel rising to 2,500 feet; and Tusculum (Frascati), peeping out from its woodlands over the Tiber valley.

Two natural lines of communication extended from end to end of Latium. A lower route, along which the Romans eventually laid out their most famous trunk road, the Via Appia, ran straight across the coastal plain after a rise and fall over the foot-hills of the Alban Mount; the upper route ascended from the Tiber valley to the low col of Mons Algidus and followed the easy reverse slope into the basin of the Liris. The latter route had the advantage of rising well above inundation level, and it was along this line that the earliest of Roman military highways, the Via Latina, was constructed.

The facility of internal communications across Latium and the need for common defence, whether against the Etruscans across the Tiber or against the peoples of the Apennine border (the Aequi to the north and the Volsci to the east), pointed to an early association of the Latin communities. In the sixth century, if not earlier, a political league had been formed *ad caput Ferentinae* [at the source of the Ferentine waters], at an unidentified point beneath the Alban mount; but it was disrupted (probably *c.* 500 B.C.) by a thrust of the Volscians across the Liris valley to the coast, and never restored in its completeness. Contrary to the indications of geography, the political leadership of Latium was eventually assumed by the border town of Rome. But this city was marked out by Nature to achieve a dominion far wider than over Latium, and it was able to take Latium, as it were, in its stride.

The site on which the city of Rome stood bore little resemblance to the usual location of an early Greek or Italian town. Instead of being built compactly on and around a single dominating eminence, it sprawled over a tumbled area of small bluffs and intersecting valleys. The explanation of this abnormality is that Rome was an afterthought. The city was the product of an amalgamation of earlier village settlements on the upper ranges of the several hills. Though these heights in no case exceeded 200 feet above sea-level, they rose for the most part in steep slopes above the surrounding valleys, and at some points presented sheer cliffs to them; and the valleys served for part of the year as ditches, for it required extensive draining and embanking operations before they were rendered immune from the Tiber floods. But although the hills formed natural strongholds, they were of too narrow compass to offer refuge to any considerable population—the summit of the Palatine extended over twenty-five acres only, and that of the Capitoline over a mere twenty; and the defensive position of the city of Rome as a whole was by no means formidable.

But if Rome was not a natural fortress, it possessed the far greater advantage of being a natural centre of communications such as no other city of Italy could equal. Though its river, the Tiber, was not the largest of Italian streams—at Rome it did not exceed 100 yards in width—it carried a relatively large and equable volume of water and was the most easily navigable in its lower course. Its upper reaches served to convey to Rome a large part of the timber and stone which the city required for construction-work, and its last fifteen miles between Rome and Ostia could take sea-going vessels of light draught. The Aventine mount, at the foot of which the up-river traffic discharged, therefore became an emporium for Latium in general in the days of the Roman kings.

But if Rome possessed the largest river-port of Italy, it never attracted to itself a maritime traffic comparable to that of the principal harbours on the Italian coast. The bulk of its imports from overseas had to be transferred to lighters at the river mouth and towed to the Aventine quays by means of oxen. The seaport of Ostia, moreover, suffered from the fact that it was a mere roadstead on an open coast and was rendered more and more inaccessible by a bar formed from the river silt; as a properly equipped harbour with protected basins it did not come into existence until the time of the Emperor Claudius. In spite of its proximity to the sea, Rome could never become a world-centre of maritime trade like the chief river-ports of northwestern Europe; its foreign trade was the result rather than the cause of its imperial expansion, and it was mainly limited to its own requirements.

Rome, however, was more than a river-port. It was also a bridge-town, being situated at the lowest point of the Tiber where firm abutments for a bridge could be found, and an island in mid-channel at the most convenient locality for a bridge facilitated the spanning of the river. By possession. of this crossing-point Rome controlled the main line of communications along the western and more populous side of the peninsula.

Lastly, Rome had the advantage of a central situation within the Italian lands, being roughly equidistant (in a bee-line of c. 350 miles) from the corner points of Augusta Taurinorum, Aquileia, Brundisium, and Rhegium. It was therefore the natural starting-point of the fan-work of trunk roads across the peninsula, up the Tiber valley, through the Umbrian and Marsic gaps of the Apennine chain, down the river Liris, and along the Latin coast. As a river-port, bridge-town, and focusing-point of roads, Rome equalled London, and within Italy it was less eccentric than London is in Britain.

Thus Rome was marked out by Nature to be the capital of a unified Italy, just as Italy, by virtue of its large man-power and relatively central situation within the Mediterranean lands, was the natural seat of a Mediterranean empire. Rome's lordship over the ancient Mediterranean world was in accordance with the basic facts of Mediterranean geography.

Tenney Frank

ECONOMIC NECESSITY

Tenney Frank (1876–1939) attained the presidency of the American Philological Association and editorship of the *American Journal of Philology*, in addition to writing varied books and articles on Roman history and literature. He specialized in economic history, editing *An Economic Survey of Ancient Rome* (of which he wrote two volumes) and writing *An Economic History of Rome*, from which this selection is taken. This author is more concerned with trade and agriculture than with Rome's location in Italy. Does Tenney Frank's description of Latium contrast with or supplement Max Cary's description of the same area? How far can one carry an economic explanation of the rise of Rome?

ITALY's wealth in ancient times as in modern lay in her food-producing soil. Gold was never found in the peninsula, and but little silver. Iron and copper were mined only in a narrow strip of Etruria, too circumscribed to entice many Romans into industries. The commerce of the seas was developed and held by people less well endowed with productive land, races compelled to trade if they were to survive. Agriculture was therefore Italy's industry, in particular the cultivation of the Western littoral composed of the ejecta of the many volcanoes between central Etruria and Naples, and of the deep alluvial deposits of the Po valley. The hardy farmers of the Roman Campagna it was who organized the irresistible legions that united Italy and through the united strength of Italy the Mediterranean world, and it was the submersion of this stock of farmers that hastened the end of ancient civilization.

The Latin plain in its present conformation is very recent, so recent that the last masses of volcanic ash probably post-date the pyramids of Egypt. The process of formation continued from long before the glacial periods and all through them. More than fifty craters, from which the ash and lava poured, can still be found within twenty-five miles of the imperial city. Long periods of tranquility intervened when jungles grew up over the temporary surface, only to be buried under a new mass of ashes. The deep cuttings of the railways that run out of the eastern gates of Rome expose repeated layers of black and yellow soil lying between thick strata of tufa and ash; they mark the jungles of former intervals of rest. The present surface is not old. The mouth of the Tiber has apparently silted in as much alluvium since Ostia lay upon the seashore in Sulla's day as the river carried down between the last great eruptions and

From Tenney Frank, *An Economic History of Rome to the End of the Republic* (Baltimore, 1920), 1–9, 51–62, by permission of the Johns Hopkins Press.

Ostia's foundation. Though the Sabine hills immediately behind this plain show numerous sites of habitation several millennia old—some being the homes of savages of the palaeolithic age—and though there are traces throughout the peninsula of the earliest Indo-European peoples of the Terramara civilization (the men who in the third millennium introduced the use of copper), the oldest graves of the Forum, the Palatine, and of Grottaferrata cannot with certainty be placed earlier than the iron age, perhaps not more than a thousand years before Cicero. Archaeologists have doubted the accuracy of the reports published by the excavators who a century ago claimed that the burial urns uncovered below Castel Gandolfo were found under undisturbed layers of volcanic ash, but Pinza has proved the reports accurate, and his own theory that Alba Longa was buried in the debris of an Alban eruption does not entirely lack plausibility.

The Latin plain is then of very recent date, and human cultivation of it of still more recent. It is well known that the volcanic ash that falls from Vesuvius is rich in phosphates and potash and that a moderate admixture of it in the soil acts as an excellent fertilizer. In fact, the Campanian farmer living in the shadow of Vesuvius is not averse to an occasional eruption if only the volcano behaves with moderation. The later ash-strata of the Alban volcanoes had an abundance of these same constituents, though a large percentage of the original elements has leached out with time. Needless to say, however, the ash alone did not lend itself to cultivation at once, since grain needs an abundance of nitrogenous matter, and a solider soil than the ash at first provided. Before men could inhabit the Latin plain we must posit a period of wild growth and the invasion of jungle plants and forests which could create a sufficiently thick humus for agricultural purposes. Such forests did invade the plain. Not only do all the authors preserve the traditions of forests and sacred groves that are mentioned in the tales of early kings, but Theophrastus still knew of Latium as a source of timber as late as the third century: "The land of the Latins is well watered, and the plains bear the laurel and myrtle and remarkable beech trees. Trunks are found that singly suffice for the keel beams of the great Tyrrhenian ships. Fir and pine grow upon the hills. The Circaean promontory is thickly overgrown with oaks, laurels, and myrtle." It is interesting to find that the beech then grew in the Latin plains, for now that the Campagna is parched and treeless it has withdrawn to the hills, if not to the mountains.

With this growth of timber from a subsoil which had many excellent qualities, a very rich soil was being formed for farming when once the Alban volcanoes should cease pouring out the flames that kept the hill-peoples back in fear. There can be little doubt that the region was far from being semi-arid then as it is now. To-day the grass parches brown in June, not to revive again till near October, and the wheat is hurried to a premature harvest in the middle of June. But Varro sets July down as the month of harvest in his day, and summer rains are frequently mentioned in the classical authors. It would be hazardous to assume a theory of "climatic pulses" by way of explanation of this difference, and it is doubtful whether a mere two thousand years in the long recession of the glacial area could cause a perceptible change in temperature. The explanation of the change is perhaps to be found in the almost complete deforestation of Latium and the mountain behind. There can be little doubt that when the Sabine ridge from Praeneste to Monte Gennaro and the whole Volscian range were a thick forest instead of the parched white rocks that now stand out, the cool mountains when struck by the humid sirocco caused condensation and precipitation over the plain. In those days moreover, the areas of forests still standing on the mountain sides and plains retained the water long and afforded a lasting subsoil supply and an abundance of nightly dewfalls which do not now exist when the last rains of spring leap off the bare rocks and flow away at once in torrents.

When, therefore, the early settlers pushed down into the Campagna and burned out "clearings" for farming (indeed the Terramara folk had then practiced systematic agriculture in the Po valley for many centuries), they found a soil remarkably fertile, though not yet very deep, and a warmth and humidity that make the harvest rich. As was to be expected from such conditions, the population in time grew dense. There is nothing improbable in the tradition of the fifty villages that Pliny has preserved.

The treasures now being gathered into the museum of the Villa Giulia from the ruins of sixth century Ardea, Satricum, Lanuvium, Gabii, Praeneste, Nemi, Velitrae, Norba, and Signia, speak of an era of prosperity that no one dared imagine a few years ago. The ancient lords of these cities, which became malarial wastes before Cicero's day, decked themselves and their homes in the gold and precious stones of all the lands from the Baltic Sea to the Mesopotamian valley. Yet the wealth which made possible all this display did not spring from Latin industry or from commerce directed by Latins, if we may trust the archaeological evidence available. It was the produce of a rich soil cultivated with unusual intensity which paid for it, and kept alive a thick population such as would probably compare with the swarming tenantry of the Po valley of to-day.

There are numerous relics from that remarkable agricultural period still to be found in Latium, traces of drains, tunnels, and dams that are all too little known. The modern Italian farmer who hardly finds his land worth the merest labor of planting and harvesting fails to see how in a former day the owners could have secured returns for such enormous expenditure of labor. A convenient place to study the intricate draining system of that time is the district below Velitrae. Here as De La Blanchère discovered some forty years ago the ground is honeycombed with an elaborate system of tunnels running down the slopes of the hills toward the Pontine marshes, *cuniculi* as he calls them, about 3 by 1½ feet, cut in the tufa a few feet below the surface and usually along the sides of the numerous ravines. De La Blanchère was unfortunately misled by the then prevailing "miasmatic" theory of malaria into believing that these tunnels were cut to drain the soil of pest waters. But they occur only on the slopes where the land drains all too readily without aid; they do not touch the stagnant Pontine marshes below. However, he also suggested as a possible theory what seems indeed to be the true explanation. They were apparently cut at a time of such overpopulation that every foot of arable ground must be saved for cultivation. By diverting the rain waters from the eroding mountain gullies into underground channels the farmers not only checked a large part of the ordinary erosion of the hillside farms but also saved the space usually sacrificed to the torrent-bed. It would be difficult to find another place where labor has been so lavishly expended to preserve the arable soil from erosion. The ground must have been very valuable, and the population in great need to justify such heroic measures for the insurance of the annual harvest. Similar systems are found in the valleys north of Veii and were probably built under similar conditions. Indeed, the remarkable cutting seventy-five yards long at Ponte Sodo near the citadel rock of Veii through which the Fosso di Formello has ever since flowed seems to have been undertaken to save a few acres of the circling river bed for cultivation. Similarly the emissarium of the Alban lake, 1,300 yards long and 7 to 10 feet high, was cut through solid rock to save a few hundred acres of arable soil on the sloping edge within the crater. Even with the tools of modern engineers, that task would not now be considered a paying investment. Finally let the student of intensive tillage take a morning walk from Marcellina up Monte Gennaro through the steep ravine of Scarpellata. It is usually dry, but after a heavy rain the water pours down in torrents, carrying off what little soil may tend to accumulate. To save small alluvial patches in the course of this ravine the ancient farmers built elaborate dams of finely trimmed polygonal masonry that still withstand the torrents. The masonry is largely made of huge blocks weighing half a ton each and is in no wise inferior to the magnificent polygonal masonry of Segni's town walls. And yet one of these dams could hardly save more than half an acre of arable soil.

It is impossible after surveying such elaborate undertakings to avoid the conclusion that Latium in the sixth century was cultivated with an intensity that has seldom been equalled anywhere. When, furthermore, we consider that the tools of that period were the spade and the mattock, we may be sure that each man's allotment was very small, doubtless no more than the two jugera that Varro assures us sufficed for the support of the ancient Latin family. It follows that Latium supported a very densely settled population. With these facts in view the historian can understand whence came the armies that overran the limits of Latium and overwhelmed all obstruction when once they were set in motion, why Veii fell, why the

burning of Rome was so quickly repaired, and why Campania called
all the way to Rome for aid when
threatened by the Samnites. It is very
probable that when the soil began
to show signs of exhaustion under
this severe strain and an incapacity
to feed the population which is
proved by the desperate methods
mentioned above, the growing generations found it necessary to seek more
room, and that the expansion of the
Latin tribe dates from this condition.

*   *   *

The intensity of the effort to re-
claim small bits of eroding land
was a proof of overpopulation and
of a dangerous drain upon the productive qualities of the soil. The
danger of soil exhaustion was peculiarly great in Latium for several reasons. The soil there had not had a
long time for accumulation. Along
the extensive ridges of lava that
radiate from the Alban hills toward
the Anio, along the Appian way, and
down toward Ardea, the surface was
so hard that soil-making was well-
nigh impossible. In such places the
plow cannot now be driven. A mere
scratch in the thin turf exposes the
lava. In other places the conditions
were more favorable since the ash
and tufa are fairly productive for
plants of powerful roots when covered
with a humus of proper physical
consistency and containing some
nitrogenous matter. The surface was,
however, new and therefore thin
everywhere except in alluvial valleys.
To add to the unfortunate conditions,
the ash had fallen unevenly in knolls
that time has not yet shaped down

into a peneplain. In consequence the
Campagna presents to the abrading
rains of winter a very uneven surface,
and when the Latin settlers had once
stripped the turf and forest from that
surface, the thin soil was in danger
of washing away. It is not surprising
that the Latin farmer found it necessary to entice the thieving rainwater
intŏ underground channels with the
utmost speed. The surface loam was
very precious and must be saved. Not-
withstanding his efforts, however, the
exhausting harvests and the continual
erosion did their work, and Latin
agriculture was doomed, and with it
the thick adornment of prosperous
Latin villages. The situation could
well be illustrated by the history of
agriculture in the sandy districts of
central Pennsylvania, where the
traveller to-day passes through large
areas of country almost uninhabited
though well studded with barns and
farmhouses now abandoned and fall-
ing into ruin. Here the settlers of
two centuries ago found a rich but
thin alluvial soil lying over a subsoil of sand. A century of reckless
tilling drew great wealth from the
soil, but when that had been ex-
ploited the land was of little value
and the farmers left it.

The situation in Latium never
grew equally desperate, nor will it,
since the subsoil there, even though
slow to yield its wealth to the feeble
roots of mere annual vegetation, is
nevertheless comparatively rich. Yet,
to judge from the constant cries of
distress reported by the early books
of Livy, the fifth and fourth centuries
before our era were years of increasing exhaustion. To add to the
desperate situation, the extensive

forests which had insured rainfall well into the summer and had helped husband the moisture in the dry season were ever giving way to the axe. The pressing demand for land resulted in the clearing out of every tract that could be made arable; the abundant population laid large demands upon the forests for lumber; and commerce, as we have seen, carried Latin timber as far as Greece, now well stripped of trees. The deforestation of the Volscian mountains on the south of the Campagna resulted in the ruin of that whole region, for the rains washed the mountain sides clear of soil, carried down the detritus into the flat plain below, choked up the course of the streams and turned what was once the garden spot of several large cities into malarial marshes, a pest not only to its own dwindling population but also to villages as far off as Satricum and Astura. Norba, Cora, Setia, and Privernum dwindled down to unimportant hamlets. The same process of deforestation of the Sabine hills turned these also into bare rocks. Precipitation decreased, the dry seasons grew in length, the rain that fell found its quick course to the sea, and Latium became gradually the semi-arid plain that it is to-day.

While this change was in process the farmers naturally sought for remedies. There was scarcity of manure because during the very intensive tillage when every acre was in use it had not been profitable to keep cattle, since beef was rarely served as food, and horses were not in general use. When, however, many farmers found the loam too thin for further cultivation they had no choice but to seed their fields into pasture land, since turf could·at least protect whatever loam remained. A few oxen were needed as draft animals, and the wealthy lords of the city provided some market for the meat. Sheep were also in demand for wool, though this had generally come by barter from the mountain pastures that were fit only for sheep-raising. Goats might be raised for milk and cheese.

The chief difficulty for the shepherd and herdsman was the lack of grass in August and September, which necessitated the laborious work of cutting leaves from trees. However, in the fourth and third centuries, when the neighboring mountain pastures of the Volscian and the Sabine hills fell within the political sphere of Rome, a profitable combination of summer and winter pastures became possible. Whether it was the Latin landlord who sought to tide over the arid summer by resorting to the mountain pastures in dry season, or whether it was, as in the middle of the nineteenth century, the Sabine flock owners who discovered green and warm winter pasturage for their flocks in the abandoned farms of the Campagna, we do not now know. But when once the discovery was made the Latin landlords were quick to seize the opportunity to find a now profitable use for the land that would no longer yield a reasonable harvest of grain. The earliest record we have of Roman slaves in great numbers shepherding on the mountains near Rome dates from the Second Punic War but since such notices are incidental and rare we need not assume that the custom was then of recent date. He who has had the misfortune of trying to make his way from Tivoli to Rome against the endless procession of sheep going mountainward during the first week of July knows well what Horace meant when he wrote:

Now the shepherd seeks the shade with his sleepy flock.

This change, however, had serious consequences. Profitable sheep- and cattle-raising required capital, if indeed pastures were to be provided in two regions; and obviously, since the shepherding of a hundred sheep required little more labor than the care of half a dozen, the poor farmer with his small plot fell quite behind in the competition. Thus the small farmers gradually yielded ground to the master who could command the capital of large-scale ranching; and a general "enclosure" movement began at the expense of the grain fields. Again, since little skill was required, slaves were bought to care for the herds, and henceforth an area of a thousand acres, which in the days of profitable tillage had supported a hundred peasant families, now fell to the charge of a few foreign slaves living at random. The depopulation of the Campagna proceeded apace.

Another industry presently hurried the process of crowding agriculture out of the Alban region. Here the abrasion of the soil had been most rapid because the slopes were steeper, but it was discovered that while the weak roots of annual plants like wheat and barley could no longer cope with the soil, grape vines and olive trees could readily nourish themselves even in the tufa and ash that

remained. All that is necessary is to hack out and crush the tufa and plant the roots deep with a handful of loam for the plant to feed upon when young. When the plant grows strong it finds its own nourishment where grain fails in the struggle. From that time to this the vineyards and olive groves have never disappeared from the hills and valleys about the Alban lake. Obviously this industry also was developed by the men of wealth who could afford to wait five years for the first vintage and fifteen years for the first returns on their investment in the olive groves.

It is customary to say that when Rome gained possession of Sicily in the first Punic war and thus inherited from Carthage the grain tithes of that island she destroyed agriculture in Latium by flooding the market of the Latin farmer with cheap grain. But is it probable that the Roman landlords, who after all controlled the State, would have adopted a policy so ruinous to their own interests? Or is it likely that they were so stupid as not to see that this would be the result of bringing the Sicilian tithes to Rome? Is it not far more reasonable to suppose that the process we have sketched had actually progressed far by the middle of the third century, that Latium had already become a failure as a grainland, that the landlords had already turned to other industries, and that Sicilian grain filled a need already keenly felt?

The momentous changes here sketched in brief compass were the work of a long period from the fifth to the second century. They necessitated of course a constant re-shifting of a population which we have found reason to believe was very dense in the sixth century. A similar exhaustion of the soil in Greece somewhat earlier had driven large hordes to colonize foreign lands and had turned many into commercial and industrial enterprises which revolutionized such cities as Athens and Corinth. Rome sought neither remedy directly. Her citizens did not abandon Rome for foreign lands, nor did Rome turn to manufacturing and commerce, although there seem to be signs in the building of Ostia and in the legislation of Appius Claudius that there was for a while a tendency in that direction. The surplusage of Roman population found an outlet instead in the territorial expansion which set in under the vigorous democratic leaders that came to the fore in the middle of the fourth century, soon after the plebeians had won their contest for the consulship in 366. In 343 the Romans aided the Campanians in driving back the Samnite mountaineers. The war resulted after two years in an allied victory through which Rome received some territory north of Campania for colonization. The year after this war the Latin peoples revolted from Rome's hegemony and, being defeated, were incorporated into the Roman state, part as full citizens, part for a probationary period as non-voting citizens. There were of course losses of men on both sides, and some land was confiscated and settled by Romans. In 328 a new Samnite war broke out which gradually spread through the whole of central Italy including the Etruscans, Umbrians, and Sa-bine peoples. For forty years there was almost constant warfare. This was finally followed by the war with Pyrrhus whose defeat left Rome the recognized leader of a federation extending from the Arno throughout the whole of Italy.

This era of territorial expansion followed as we have seen a period of over-population and land hunger which had expressed itself constantly in a clamor for economic and social amelioration. Historians who have written of the period have always been disposed to conclude that land hunger was the driving force which led to the expansion. Possibly this conclusion is correct. There can be no doubt of the desire for more land. An agricultural people when hard pressed economically thinks in terms of territorial expansion, and the Romans though very legalistic were as quick as many other peoples have been to take mortal offense at a neighbor's behavior when they need their neighbor's food. However, we have no right to be induced to this conclusion either by the short-circuited argument of *post hoc ergo*, nor by an *a priori* faith in the economic interpretation of history. It is only fair to point out first that the Roman people who had for centuries to defend their titles to desirable plain-lands against the inroads of hungry mountaineers had thereby developed to a maximum the low-lander's sense of property rights and justice. It is not by mere chance that Rome's civil code has been adopted by all the world as the basis of law. Moreover a careful study of Rome's method of utilizing her victories reveals the behavior not of a land-hungry bandit but of a far-seeing political organizer. A parcel of land was often appropriated by way of indemnity, and it was frequently a fertile plot which would invite and retain its colonists, but the individual portions were generally very small, just sufficient for a military post, and among the settlers was always included a fair proportion of the allied peoples. The new settlements of the fourth century show unmistakably that the government kept needs of the state foremost, not the cry of citizens for new allotments. The first settlements were made at the seaport towns of Antium and Tarracina which had exposed Latium to the raids of sea rovers, and of Greek and Etruscan fleets. But only three hundred men were sent to each, enough presumably to take political control and command the ports; and the allotments consisted of a few acres per man. Colonists were next settled on some land of Privernum to control the pass over the Volscian mountains behind Tarracina, land which was too exposed to the malaria of the Pontine marshes to be chosen as highly desirable for economic reasons. Above Capua in the territory taken from the Sidicini, allies of the Samnites, the Latin colony of Cales was planted. It contained 2,500 settlers, partly Romans who gave up their citizenship for the Latin status, and partly Latin and Campanian allies. Cales in fact is an instance of the typical border colony that Rome favored. Good enough land was chosen to induce the settlers to remain and guard a perilous spot, Romans and allies were mingled in recognition of mutual rights and to serve as a cohesive group in the federation, and the situation was selected chiefly for its strategic value: Cales guarded the inner road between Rome and Capua, and it separated the Samnites from the newly subjected Aurunci. Similar military colonies were planted at Luceria, Suessa, Interamna and Alba. Finally the Falernian fields above Cumae where the coast road debouches into Campania was taken and settled by Roman citizens. The reason for the appropriation was partly strategic, partly punitive, for the inhabitants, apparently an old enclave of Etruscans, had aided the Samnites against Rome. The land was indeed excellent, but had good land been the chief concern, Rome need not have sent her citizens one hundred miles away.

These are the settlements made in the period of expansion during the fourth century and they are fairly representative of Rome's policy for the next century as well. The only difference is that in the third century the settlement of Romans alone is of infrequent occurrence, the Latin military colony becomes the standard type, and some lands, such as the Ager Gallicus, fail for a long time to find takers. These are all indications that by the third century Rome suffered not from land hunger but from a scarcity of men needed for her task.

An adequate statement of how far Rome's expansion was conditioned by economic pressure it would be hazardous to attempt without a complete review of the whole history of Rome's foreign policy. The close connection between the economic revolution and the political expansion cannot be denied. We may at least say that the overpopulation of Latium apparent in the early period and the distress of the people due to a gradual deterioration of the soil played an important part in setting into activity the instincts and impulses which led the government into an aggressive foreign policy in 343; subsequent ventures, and the possession of a dense population of farmers enabled the government to build up an irresistible army which made conquest relatively easy. The wastage of the wars however and the requirements for military colonies at strategic points soon absorbed the surplusage to such an extent that the third century discloses an insufficiency rather than a congestion of population. Furthermore the evidence shows clearly that the government from the beginning was controlled by a well-ordered policy which considered political and military needs paramount and that it never betrayed these to the exigencies of the economic pressure exerted through individual citizens.

It is equally manifest however that the political expansion of Rome reacted permanently upon the economic life of the people. The constant availability of good lands which the state desired to have occupied against possible encroachment always attracted men and capital not otherwise occupied. Thus the Romans now felt no incentive to try new enterprises, to develop industries or to enter commerce on land or sea.

III. CHARACTER OF THE ROMANS

R. H. Barrow

ORDER THROUGH REVERENCE

R. H. Barrow is a British classicist and historian. He is currently on the staff of the *Oxford Latin Dictionary* now in preparation. His many works on the ancient world include *The Romans* and *Plutarch and His Times*. He finds the Romans' unwavering subordination to authority, especially to religious authority, to be the key to their success. Would such conformity foster the development of brilliant political and military leaders, such as Rome certainly had at times?

THROUGHOUT their history the Romans were acutely aware that there is "power" outside man, individually or collectively, of which man must take account. He must subordinate himself to something. If he refuses, he invites disaster; if he subordinates himself unwillingly, he becomes the victim of superior force; if willingly, he finds that he may be raised to the rank of cooperator; by cooperation he can see something of the trend, even the purpose, of that superior power. Willing cooperation gives a sense of dedication; the purposes become clearer, and he feels he is an agent or an instrument in forwarding them; at a higher level he becomes conscious of a vocation, of a mission for himself and for men like him, who compose the state. When the Roman general celebrated his "triumph" after a victorious campaign, he progressed through the city from the gates to the temple of Jupiter (later in imperial times to the temple of Mars Ultor) and there offered to the god "the achievements of Jupiter wrought *through* the Roman people."

From the earliest days of Rome we can detect in the Roman a sense of dedication, at first crude and inarticulate and by no means unaccompanied by fear. In later days it is clearly expressed and is often a mainspring of action. In the latest days the mission of Rome is clearly proclaimed; it is often proclaimed most loudly by men who strictly were not Romans, and most insistently at the very time when in its visible expression the mission was accomplished. The sense of dedication at first reveals itself in humble forms, in the household and in the family; it is enlarged in the city-state and it finds its culmination in the imperial idea. From time to time it employs different categories of thought and modes of expression; but in its essence it is religious, for it is a leap beyond experience. When the mission is accomplished, its basis changes.

From R. H. Barrow, *The Romans* (Harmondsworth, England, 1949), 9–14, 21–26, 215–216. Reprinted by permission of Penguin Books, Ltd.

This is the clue to Roman character and to Roman history.

The Roman mind is the mind of the farmer and soldier; not farmer, nor soldier, but farmer-soldier; and this is true on the whole even in the later ages when the Roman might be neither farmer nor soldier. "Unremitting work" is the lot of the farmer, for the seasons wait for no man. Yet his own work by itself will achieve nothing; he may plan and prepare, till and sow; in patience he must await the aid of forces which he cannot understand, still less control. If he can make them favourable, he will; but most often he can only cooperate, and he places himself in line with them that they may use him as their instrument, and so he may achieve his end. Accidents of weather and pest may frustrate him; he must accept compromise and be patient. Routine is the order of his life; seed-time, growth, and harvest follow in appointed series. The life of the fields is his life. If as a citizen he is moved to political action at last, it will be in defence of his land or his markets or the labour of his sons. To him the knowledge born of experience is worth more than speculative theory. His virtues are honesty and thrift, forethought and patience, work and endurance and courage, self-reliance, simplicity, and humility in the face of what is greater than himself.

Such also are the virtues of the soldier. He too will know the value of routine, which is a part of discipline, for he must respond as by instinct to a sudden call. He must be self-reliant. The strength and endurance of the farmer serve the soldier; his practical skill helps him to become what the Roman soldier must be, a builder and a digger of ditches and maker of roads and ramparts. He lays out a camp or a fortification as well as he lays out a plot or a system of drains. He can live on the land, for that is what he has done all his life. He too knows the incalculable element which may upset the best of dispositions. He is conscious of unseen forces, and he attributes "luck" to a successful general whom some power—destiny or fortune—uses as an instrument. He gives his loyalty to persons and to places and to friends. If he becomes politically violent, he will be violent to secure, when the wars are over, land to till and a farm to live in; and still greater loyalty rewards the general who champions his cause. He has seen many men and many places, and with due caution he will imitate what he has seen to work; but for him "that corner of the earth smiles above all others," his home and native fields, and he will not wish to see them changed.

The study of Roman history is, first, the study of the process by which Rome, always conscious of her dedication, painfully grew from being the city-state on the Seven Hills until she became mistress of the world; secondly, the study of the means by which she acquired and maintained that dominion; the means was her singular power of turning enemies into friends, and eventually into Romans, while yet they remained Spaniards or Gauls or Africans. From her they derived "Romanitas," their "Roman-ness." "Romanitas" is a convenient word used by the Christian Tertullian to mean all that a Roman takes for granted, the Roman point of view and habit of thought. It is akin to "Roman civilization" only upon a strict view of what civilization is. Civilization is what men think and feel and do and the values which they assign to what they think and feel and do. It is true that their creative thoughts and their standards of feeling and value may issue in acts which profoundly affect the use which they make of material things; but "material civilization" is the least important aspect of civilization, which really resides in men's minds. As Tacitus said, it is the ignorant (and he was speaking of the Britons) who think that fine buildings and comforts and luxuries make up civilization. The Latin word here used (*humanitas*) was a favourite word with Cicero, and the conception behind it was peculiarly Roman and was born of Roman experience. It means, on the one side, the sense of the dignity of one's own human personality, which is a thing unique and which must be cared for and developed to the full; on the other side, it means a recognition of the personalities of others and their right to care for their own personalities; and this recognition implies compromise and self-restraint and sympathy and consideration.

But the usual and more concrete phrase for civilization is simply "the Roman peace." It was in this idea that the world found it easiest to see the fulfilment of that mission which Roman character and experience and power had gradually brought to the upper levels of consciousness and had deliberately discharged. In the earliest days of the Roman people its leader solemnly took the "auspices" by observation of signs revealed through religious rites, to discover whether the action which the state proposed to take was in line with the gods' will, which ruled the world. Cicero, enumerating the fundamental principles upon which the state rests, places first "religion and the auspices," and by "auspices" he means that unbroken succession of men from Romulus onwards to whom was given the duty to discover the gods' will. The "auspices" and the sacred colleges, the Vestal Virgins and the rest, find their place in the letters of Symmachus, born A.D. 340, who was a tenacious leader of pagan opposition to Christianity, the "official" religion of the Empire. Cicero it is who says that the birth of Roman power, its increase and its maintenance, are due to Roman religion; Horace says that subordination to the gods has given the Roman his empire. Four centuries later St Augustine devotes the first part of his most powerful book to wrestling with the prevalent faith that the greatness of Rome had been due to pagan gods, and that salvation from the threatening doom was to be found in them. It may well be said, in the words of the Greek Polybius, 205–123 B.C., himself a sceptic, "What more than anything else distinguishes the Roman state and sets it above all others is its attitude to the gods. It seems to me that what is a reproach to other communities actually holds together the Roman state—I mean its awe of the gods," and he uses the same word which St Paul used on Mars' Hill in Athens. Polybius was not to know that at the very end, when the Roman Empire was overrun by barbarians, it would be the idea of the greatness and eternity of Rome which would hold together belief in the gods.

* * *

Later ages looked back to the primitive simplicity of early times, and no doubt idealized it. But it was not myth; in the third and second century B.C. there was literature which testified to it, for men then wrote who had come in contact with men who had been thus brought up. The "old ways" survived as realities, and still more as ideals. If we enumerate some of the virtues which Romans regarded as characteristically Roman throughout their history, we must connect them with the native endowment, the pursuits and manner of life, the early struggles for survival, and the religion of the first centuries of the Republic. They will be seen to be all of a piece.

First in every catalogue of virtues comes some recognition that a man should admit his subordination to something external which has a "binding-power" upon him, and the term for this, *religio*, has a wide application. For a "religious man" the phrase is usually "a man of the highest *pietas*," and *pietas* is part of that subordination of which we have spoken. You are *pius* to the gods if you admit their claims: you are *pius* to your parents and elders, and children and friends, and country and benefactors, and all that excites, or should excite, your regard and perhaps affection, if you admit their claims on you, and discharge your duty accordingly; the claims exist because the relationships are sacred. The demands of *pietas* and of

officium (duty and services, as in "tender offices") constituted in themselves a massive and unwritten code of feeling and behaviour which was outside the law, and was so powerful as to modify in practice the harsh rules of private law, which were only a last resort.

Gravitas means "a sense of the importance of the matters in hand," a sense of responsibility and earnestness. It is a term to apply at all levels—to a statesman or a general as he shows appreciation of his responsibilities, to a citizen as he casts his vote with consciousness of its importance, to a friend who gives his advice based on his experience and on regard for your welfare; Propertius uses it when assuring his mistress of "the seriousness of his intentions." It is the opposite of *levitas*, a quality the Romans despised, which means trifling when you should be serious, flippancy, instability. *Gravitas* is often joined with *constantia*, firmness of purpose, or with *firmitas*, tenacity; it may be seasoned with *comitas*, which means the relief given to over-seriousness by ease of manner, good humour, and humour. *Disciplina* is the training which provides steadiness of character; *industria* is hard work; *virtus* is manliness and energy; *clementia* the willingness to forgo one's rights; *frugalitas*, simple tastes.

These are some of the qualities which Romans most admired. They are moral qualities; they may even be dull and unexciting. There is nothing among them to suggest that intellectual power, or imaginativeness, or sense of beauty, or versatility, or charm—that hard-worked word nowadays—appealed to them as a high ideal. The qualities which served the Roman in his early struggles with Nature and with neighbours remained for him the virtues above all others. To them he owed it that his city-state had risen superior to the older civilization which surrounded it—a civilization which appeared to him to be limp and nerveless unless stiffened by the very virtues which he himself had painfully cultivated. Perhaps they can be summed up under *severitas,* which means being stern with oneself.

The manner of life and the qualities of character here described make up the *mores maiorum,* the manners of one's ancestors, which are among the most potent forces in Roman history. In the broadest sense the phrase may include the political constitution and the legal framework of the state, though generally such words as *instituta,* institutions, and *leges,* laws, are added. In the narrower sense the phrase means the outlook on life, the moral qualities, together with the unwritten rules and precedents of duty and behaviour, which combined to form a massive tradition of principle and usage. To this tradition appeal was made when revolutionaries laid violent hand on political practice, on religious custom, or on standards of morality or taste. The constancy of this appeal, made by orator and poet, soldier and statesman, showed that it had not lost its force even in the most troubled times or in the latest ages. Reformers might ignore tradition, but they could not deride it; and no Roman dreamed of destroying what was old merely because it was old. From the end of the Second Punic War, beneath the reverence

for the noble Romans who embodied this noble tradition, a new note begins to be heard—the note of regret at the passing of something of value which is too remote from the present corrupt age to be restored. It begins in Ennius, 239–169 B.C., who has been described as the Chaucer of Roman poetry, "Rome stands built upon the ancient ways of life and upon her men." Cicero, whose appeal to the *mores maiorum* is incessant and sincere, receives from Brutus the compliment that for "his virtues he could be compared with any of the ancients." No higher praise can be given to a woman than to describe her as "of the old standards of life," *antiqui moris.* Horace, whose affectionate tribute to his father is genuine, says of his own upbringing,

"Wise men," he'd add, "the reasons will explain
Why you should follow this, from that refrain:
For me, if I can train you in the ways
Trod by the worthy folks of earlier days,
And, while you need direction, keep your name
And life unspotted, I've attained my aim:
When riper years have seasoned brain and limb,
You'll drop your corks and like a Triton swim."

The tradition lived, at least as an ideal, to the last days of the Empire.

Looking back, we cannot say that a religion such as the old Roman religion was likely to promote greatly the religious development of man; it carried no intellectual appeal and was, therefore, unable to contribute a theology. But it is certain that with the associations and habits which clustered round it its contribution to Roman character was very great; by it, too, a mould was fashioned in which later ages tended to cast the new and formless mixture of ideas which reached them from the older Mediterranean cultures. Great men were almost canonized for their characters or for their achievements. To the beliefs and manners of those days we must ascribe that sense of subordination or obedience to exterior power, whether a god, or a standard, or an ideal, which in one form or another marked the Roman to the end. To the same source must be traced the feeling for continuity which, while assimilating the new, preserved the type and refused to break with the past; for the future could be faced with greater security if the value of the past were conserved. The early practice of rite accompanied by formal invocations and crystallized into a "sacred law" helped to develop that genius in law which is Rome's great legacy; and the law of the state borrowed a reflected sanctity from its sacred counterpart. Law presupposed obedience and was not disappointed. The position of the head of the family, the respect given to the mother, the training given to the children, were confirmed and strengthened. The validity of moral ideas was securely established, and ties of natural affection and of service to friends and dependants were made firm by a code of behaviour which lay outside legal obligation and was of compelling power. The formal nature of religious observance preserved Roman religion from the gross manifestations of Oriental ecstasy, even if it forbade warmth of personal feeling; and the attitude of toleration towards religion which marked the republican and imperial ages originated, paradoxically, with a people who assigned the utmost importance to state religion.

The result of the religious, moral, and political tradition of Rome was a stability of character which eventually assured the stability of the Roman world; and it should not pass unnoticed that a people, whose nature it was to look backwards, itself moved forward and placed progress within the power of others.

* * *

In a thousand years the Romans had been schooled as no other nation, and they had kept that sense of subordination. None the less, no other nation achieved an Empire so far-reaching and so fundamentally humane. Through obedience comes power. The great gift of Roman obedience flowered in due time into the great ideals of Roman law. By learning at infinite cost that lesson Rome has set those ideals upon succeeding ages. The Romans were "a law-inspired nation," but the law was of their making and they imposed it on themselves. And, as the fundamental ideas of that law are studied, they will be found to enshrine the ideals and qualities which the Romans of the earliest times set before themselves, now broadened and refined and made of universal application. Respect for eternal values, the will of the gods (*pietas*), and their expression as objective "right" in the practical things of human life—respect for human personality and human relationships (*humanitas*), whether in the family or the state or the circle of friends, springing from a regard for the personality of each individual and issuing in the maintenance of his freedom (*libertas*)—respect for tradition (*mores*) that holds fast to what has been handed down because it contains accumulated wisdom which no one moment and no one man can supply—respect for authority (*auctoritas*), not as obedience to superior power, but as regard for the judgement of men whose experience and knowledge deserve respect—respect for the pledged word (*fides*) and the expressed intention, the faith of the Romans by which "with their friends and such as relied on them they kept amity," and "the most sacred thing in life."

Respect for these things presupposed training (*disciplina*), the training of the home, of public life, of life itself, and the training which comes from the self (*severitas*). And training of this kind creates a responsible cast of mind (*gravitas*) which assigns importance to important things, so that, when once the hand is placed to the plough, a man does not look back and falter, but keeps to his purpose (*constantia*). These are the qualities which make up the genius of the Roman people.

Guglielmo Ferrero

ORDER THROUGH REGIMENTATION

Born in Italy in 1871, Guglielmo Ferrero was more a popularizer and journalist than a historian. Because he opposed Fascism, his books were banned in Italy in 1935 and he died in exile in Geneva in 1942. He wrote about many subjects, ranging from classical antiquity to modern times, and made ancient history popular reading for Italians of his own day. When Ferrero visited the Americas he was awed by and perhaps envious of the New World's growing prosperity. Is it possible that Ferrero's comparison of Europe and the Americas led him to think of the Romans as mediocre farmers? In spite of the possible reasons for his opinions, does Ferrero have a more realistic view of the early Romans than Barrow? Which view is more valid?

IN the second half of the fifth century before Christ Rome was still an aristocratic community of free peasants, occupying an area of nearly 400 square miles, with a population, certainly not exceeding 150,000, almost entirely dispersed over the countryside and divided into seventeen districts or rural Tribes. Most of the families had a small holding and cottage of their own, where father and sons lived and worked together, growing corn for the most part, with here and there a strip of vine or olive. Their few head of cattle were kept at pasture on the neighbouring common land; their clothes and simple implements of husbandry they made for themselves at home. Only at rare intervals and on special occasions would they make their way into the fortified town which was the centre at once of their religion and their government. Here were the temples of the gods, the houses of the wealthy, and the shops of the artisans and traders, where corn, oil or wine could be bartered in small quantities for salt or rough tools and weapons of iron. Every Roman landowner was assigned according to his means to one of five classes, which were further subdivided into Centuries; by contributing his vote to the vote of his Century, which counted for one in the Assembly of the Centuries or *Comitia Centuriata*, he took part in legislation and in the election of the chief magistrates of the Republic.

Yet although all the State offices were elective the constitution of Rome was doubly aristocratic. As they ascended from the poorer to the richer classes, the Centuries contained a proportionately smaller number of electors; and the higher magistracies were by a hereditary privilege reserved for a small number of patri-

From Guglielmo Ferrero, *The Greatness and Decline of Rome* (New York: G. P. Putnam Sons, 1909), I, 1–11, 13–15, 17–19.

cian families, who could boast the possession of wider lands, more numerous herds and a certain number of slaves. The sons of Senators, together with plebeians of sufficient wealth and distinction, formed a separate order, intermediate between nobility and plebs. They were recognised by the State as Knights, and amongst their other privileges was that of serving in the cavalry in time of war. The plebeians too had organisations and privileges of their own. They held local meetings in their districts for the discussion of their particular interests: and every year they appointed Tribunes of the People, whose persons were inviolable, and who had the power of putting a veto upon any action of the magistrates. Moreover, the Assembly of the Centuries had a rival in the Assembly of the Tribes, a body consisting of all who were enrolled in the seventeen rural Tribes and in the four city Tribes which comprised the scanty voting population of Rome. The Tribes superseded the Centuries, not only for the election of some of the less important magistrates, but for the transaction of current affairs. The chief power, however, still rested with the patricians, who were peasants like their fellows, and not above handling the pick and the plough. The ordinary patrician dwelling was small and rude, their fare homely, and their clothes of the simplest; they possessed little of the precious metals, and almost everything that they needed, both in food and clothing, was made at home by their womenfolk and slaves.

It was little enough, therefore, that Rome required to buy from abroad. Terracottas for the decoration of her public buildings and some imports of metal came in from Etruria, Phœnicia and Carthage, besides ivory work and ornaments, perfumes for funerals, purple for the ceremonial robes of the magistrates, and a few slaves. It was not difficult to pay for these in exports; timber for shipbuilding and salt practically made up the list. The city itself was small and poor; even the rich patricians spent most of their time in the country, and came to town only for their official duties or to attend the sittings of the Senate, of which past magistrates, on the nomination at first of the Consuls and later of the Censors, were made life members. The power of the Senate included the superintendence of the magistrates, the administration of the treasure, the ratification of the laws and elections made by the Assemblies of the Centuries and the Tribes, and the discussion of the not infrequent question of peace and war.

For the whole of Italy, up to Liguria, Emilia, and the Romagna, which were still, like the Po Valley, peopled by tribes of savage Celts and Ligurians, was dotted with fortified strongholds similar to Rome itself, guarding the course of the rivers, keeping watch over the countryside from their rough hill-tops, barring the clefts of the mountains, or standing up as far-seen landmarks to the trader in his small vessel out at sea. The constitution of these small hill-communities was sometimes aristocratic and sometimes popular, but very seldom monarchical; each possessed a certain extent of territory; and many of them formed part of confederations drawn together by race or language—such as that of the Osco-Sabellians in the South, of the Latins, Etruscans and Umbrians in Central Italy, and of the groups of Greek colonies along the coast, with their centres at Ancona, Taranto and Naples. But these forms of union were of little avail to keep the peace. All through the peninsula, from township to township, between the upland and the plain, the river valleys and the sea, there was a continual warfare between tribe and tribe. It was fed by all the incitements that rouse savage races to arms in every age—the demand for more land and slaves, the desire for precious metals, the spirit of adventure and ambition among the chiefs or a fighting temper among the people, and the urgent necessity for aggression as a security against attack and annihilation.

Like the townships all round her, Rome too had become involved in this interminable contest. Indeed, she was exposed to even greater dangers than the majority of her neighbours. Though she had succeeded in grouping about her in a confederation the small rural republics of Latium which shared her Latin tongue, she still remained in a condition of perilous weakness. Her army consisted simply of her small proprietors in arms, under the command of their wealthier neighbours: for the man who owned no land had not the right to be a soldier. All landowners between the ages of seventeen and forty-six—and these at the middle of the fifth century B.C. must have numbered about 30,000—were obliged to present themselves before the Consul whenever a levy was proclaimed, ready to be grouped into legions and to take

the field under the orders of their patrician magistrates.

But a bitter hostility was gradually growing up between rich and poor. The population of their small territory was increasing too fast, and continual wars brought ruin and devastation in their train, while the excessive cultivation of cereals was slowly exhausting the richness of the soil. Moreover, the unfortunate small landowners were being burdened with debt; while the nobility, whose numbers were increasing at an equal rate, continued to appropriate to themselves the best of the lands taken from the enemy, and to increase their herds of cattle on the public pastures, till they gradually deprived the poor altogether of their use. They had also been tempted into a practice which led to far-reaching abuses; they lent money at usury to the poorer proprietors and then reduced them to slavery on non-payment, in accordance with the ancient law of *nexum*.* There was enmity too between the rich plebeians and the patricians; for the plebeians were still jealously excluded from the magistracies. All this led to constant quarrels and rioting between the different factions, sometimes even to a temporary split in the State, which not even the imminence of war was always able to appease.

Yet once at the head of the Latin Confederation, Rome gradually brought the other towns and confederations of Italy within her power. The cause of her success lay in the vigorous discipline of her Constitution, which was strong enough to control that spirit of self-indulgence

* *Nexum:* by which a debtor pledged his liberty as security for his debt [Editor's note].

which is the most powerful solvent of national life. It was this that maintained a pure and simple morality among her rich and powerful class, which would have been the first to succumb to the vanity and vice that too frequently attend on the pride of conquest.

The Romans were a primitive people without the defects peculiar to a primitive people. This was what enabled them to conquer nations more civilised than themselves which had been weakened by the temptations incident to their superior culture. Ancient Roman society may perhaps fitly be compared to life in one of the monastic orders in the middle ages. Both systems display the same methodical combination of example and precept, of mutual vigilance and unremitting discipline. Both show us a community in which the individual is entirely at the mercy of the feelings and opinions of his fellows, and where it is impossible for him to become emancipated from the tyranny of the group. Both succeeded in drawing out from their members, in the narrow sphere allotted to their labours, an energy, a devotion and a self-control far greater than could be expected from any one of them in his individual capacity. In early Rome, everything conspired to maintain and increase among the upper classes the influence of this powerful and minutely organised system. We find it in the distribution of wealth, in religion, in the public institutions, in the severity of the legal code: we find it in a public opinion which demanded a relentless exercise of authority by fathers against their children or by husbands against their wives. We find it above all in the family, which gave the earliest and most deep-felt lessons in this stern and difficult discipline of the spirit.

The Roman family was at this time in many ways still a relic of the patriarchal age; each household was a miniature absolutism that had survived the incoming of the aristocratic republic and adapted itself to the new needs of the age. Much of the effort required to maintain the moral and political order of society could be exerted, more efficiently than by the official magistrates, within the narrow circle of family authority. Thus, in fact if not in name, the household was a real and very necessary organ of government. The father was an absolute monarch in his own house; he alone could buy or sell, hold property or make contracts. He could exact as full an obedience from his son as from his servant, whatever the age or office he had attained. He could turn a rebellious child from his door, reduce him to penury, sell him as a slave or condemn him to work in the fields; he could claim childlike obedience from a Consul who returned home from a victorious campaign. He was supreme judge over wife, children, grandchildren and slaves; and the stern ordinance of custom might even require him to send them to their death for an offence against the family, or a neighbour, or the State.

With powers such as these it was for a long time easy for parents, as each new generation grew up, to repress that youthful spirit of innovation which is in all ages the main source both of perversion and of progress; to train up their children in their own image and likeness; to accustom the boys to reverence and purity, to labour and sobriety, to the careful observance of laws and customs and of a narrow but tenacious patriotism, and to instruct them in the main precepts of domestic economy and agriculture; to teach the girls to live always under the authority of a man, whether father, husband or guardian, without the right to possess property, not even a dowry, to be gentle, obedient, and chaste, attentive only to housework and children; and to inculcate, in boys and girls alike, a scrupulous reverence for tradition, a loyal devotion to the old morality, and a horror of all innovation or luxury. It was the family which taught even the richer Roman, from the days of his youth, to be content with small enjoyments, to keep pride and vanity in check, to own submission, not to another man like himself—for monarchy he abhorred with a fanatical loathing—but to the impersonal authority of law and custom. It was the family too which taught him how to enjoy, and guided him safely through the years of early manhood, when man makes his selection among the pleasures of life according to the accidents of education and character, holding fast later to the life he has chosen with a contempt born of ignorance for all that he has rejected. And woe betide the disobedient or rebellious! Father and family tribunal would chastise son or wife without mercy; since both tradition and example counselled strictness, and it is easy for a judge to be severe when from the days of his own childhood he has known but little indulgence.

After this education, the noble Roman, still in his early manhood, gained his first experience of war through service in the cavalry: and before long he married a wife who bought him a small dowry and was to bear him many children. Then he began his long and gradual career of public life, coming before the people as a candidate for the different elective offices, according to the order prescribed by law. But no one could hope to win the suffrages of the people or the subsequent approval of the Senate unless he were known to be a respecter of tradition. And even in office his power was strictly circumscribed. If every Roman magistrate held important prerogatives, kept a numerous retinue under his orders, and was treated with solemn and ceremonial respect, yet the governing power was divided amongst a large number of individuals, all offices were unpaid and temporary, generally lasting a year, and every holder of office was given a colleague, his equal in rank and authority, for mutual supervision: while above and controlling them all was the Senate. Thus no magistrate could violate a law or a tradition without serious cause; all were obliged to yield in turn the obedience they had claimed; and on their return to private life they could be called to account for their public actions. From the cradle to the grave a Roman was spied on without ceasing; and when, at the death of his father, the son became in his turn the absolute ruler of the household, he soon found that in the Forum, the Assembly and the Senate he was exposed to a supervision no less exacting than at home. The Censors might strike him off the roll of

Senators for evil living, the people might refuse to elect him to office, and every individual citizen was a potential accuser.

Thanks to this discipline of her upper classes, Rome was able to succeed where the Etruscans had failed, and to rise little by little above the other States of Italy. In the second half of the fifth century, and the early decades of the fourth century B.C., Rome, at the head of the Latin League, engaged in a series of wars against the Æqui, Volsci and Etruscans, which enabled her, not only, in 387, to institute four new tribes on her enlarged territory, but also to found several Latin colonies on 270,000 acres of good land taken from the enemy. In this way many young men of the middle class, whose means might otherwise have debarred them from marriage, became citizens and proprietors in a new city, governed by laws of its own on the Roman model, and subject only to the obligation that her citizens should serve with the Roman legions. Encouraged by these first successes Rome was led on, during the end of the fourth and the first half of the third century, to undertake campaigns against the Samnites, Etruscans and Sabines, against the rebellious members of the Latin League, against the Gauls on the Adriatic coast, and the Greek mercenaries of Pyrrhus called in by Taranto. She thus annexed a vast territory of nearly 10,500 square miles, including the whole of Latium, part of the eastern and western districts of Tuscany, the greater part of Umbria, the Marches and Campania, reducing the cities to *municipia* and their inhabitants to citizens obliged to provide military service and the *tributum* or war tax without the privilege of a vote.

But her influence extended far beyond this area. During the whole of this time she was increasing her hold over cities and tribes in more distant parts of the peninsula. Alliances were contracted, sometimes by persuasion, sometimes by force: with Naples in 326, with Camerino, Cortona, Perugia, Arezzo, in 310, with the Marrucini, the Marsi, the Pæligni and the Frentani, in 305, with the Vestini, in 302, and afterwards with Ancona and Taranto. By the terms of these treaties the towns and tribes, while preserving their own laws and institutions, undertook to supply Rome with military contingents and to consult the Roman Senate in the case of all disputes with other States.

These wars had, in short, created a Roman Protectorate over the whole of Italy, and entailed a considerable increase in the wealth as well as in the power of Rome. Not only had the State now far greater revenues at its disposal; it had also acquired a rich domain of fields, pastures and forests all over the peninsula, part of which was let out or granted in allotments, while the rest was reserved for future needs. Many patrician and plebeian families became wealthy through the purchase of slaves and land, laying large estates under cultivation in all parts of Italy, partly in corn, partly in vine and olive, and employing "families" of slaves under the supervision of a slave foreman, helped at vintage and harvest time by free day-labourers from the nearest town. Others devoted themselves, more especially on the Common Lands of Southern Italy, to pastoral enterprise on a huge and primitive scale, not unlike what may be seen to-day in Texas and the prairie States of the American Union; their vast wandering herds of oxen and sheep, without stall or pen, grazing and sleeping under the open sky all the year round, were driven by slave shepherds every summer up to the mountains, and every winter down to the plains.

Another result of these wars was a very large increase in the supply of precious metals and in 269 or 268 B.C. Rome first coined silver money. The precious metals, always eagerly sought after by all peoples, whether barbarous or civilised, either as glittering adornments or as a form of wealth easy to carry and conceal, were in the ancient world by far the most universal object of commerce and barter, and the usual means of exchange between peoples on different levels of civilisation. Thenceforward the Romans were able to take part in international commerce, and to purchase the luxuries of Hellenic civilisation, with which, through the Greek colonies of Southern Italy, they were now brought into closer contact. Thus families of small proprietors multiplied, and lived in increased comfort, on the territory of the colonies.

But this increase of wealth did not at first tend to weaken the ancient traditions; nor was it immediately followed either by a change in manners or by a political revolution. The thrift and simplicity of the old times were still the proudest virtues of every noble family. The growth of prosperity, while it neither refined the

mass nor multiplied the enjoyments of the individual, augmented and consolidated the strength of the State, both for peace and for war. It concentrated the power in a strong military aristocracy of rich landowners, fashioned in the mould of the traditional education; and it helped to conquer new territories and to people them with Latin cultivators and Latin soldiers.

*   *   *

Thus safely shielded by the patronage of a conservative nobility the populace continued in the simple manners of their ancestors: they were still a body of sturdy and prolific yeomen, who spent the larger part of their scanty gains in bringing up new and more numerous generations of peasants and soldiers. This was the process by which, in the fourth and third centuries B.C., Rome diffused through the peninsula not merely her laws and her influence but her blood and her language: and was enabled, between 334 and 264, to found eighteen powerful Latin colonies, including Venosa, Lucera, Pæstum, Benevento, Narni, Rimini and Fermo, thus dispersing throughout the whole of Italy a race of stalwart Latin cultivators, who continued to increase on the new lands on which they settled, and to multiply the number of Latin-speaking folk amid the bewildering medley of Italian stocks and languages. These Latin yeomen devoted themselves alternately to the toil of the fields and the hardships of campaigning, regarding their pay in war time and the prize money they received from their commanders as a welcome addition to what they derived from their fields, and war itself as an industry complementary to agriculture. This continuous effort of war and conquest, lasting through several centuries, could only be successfully sustained because, thanks to the moral discipline and conservative spirit of her nobility, Rome remained, through all these campaigns, an agricultural, aristocratic and military community. The only durable conquests, even in ages of barbarism, are conquests made with the plough; the land belongs, not to adventurers who stain it with fierce and purposeless warfare, but to colonists to whom victory is but the prelude to the work of sowing and tilling and peopling the earth.

It was with these peasant soldiers that the Roman nobility formed a skeleton of cities in the body which was later to be Italy, not exhausting but extending the powers of their State. It was with these that Rome issued victorious from her first struggle with Carthage, the great trading power whose expansion brought her inevitably into collision with the military and agricultural expansion of her Italian rival; and with these that a little later, from 225–222, she waged the decisive struggle with the Gauls of Italy, which laid open to her with the conquest of the basin of the Po, the high-road of her future history.

The boundaries of her dominions were enlarged, not by any bold or comprehensive effort of genius, but by the more methodical forces of patience and tenacity. If by the end of the third century B.C. Rome had become paramount in Italy, it was because the most admired virtues in every class of her State were those that are distinctive of a well-disciplined rural community. The Roman was sober and self-restrained in all his habits and simple in all his ideas and customs. He had a deep and loving knowledge of the small world in which he lived and a quiet and imperturbable intensity of purpose. He was honest, loyal, persevering, and displayed that curious absence of excitability so characteristic of a man who has no vices, who does not waste his strength in self-indulgence, and has but a limited stock of knowledge. In such a world ideas made but slow progress; novelties, unless they came in the guise of religion, found difficult entry; genius, like madness or crime, or any other unrecognised eccentricity, was entirely suppressed; custom, experience and superstition seemed the supremest forms of wisdom. Law and religion, both strictly formal, were held in the highest honour, preserving and crystallising among their distant grandchildren the cherished beliefs that had delighted or deluded the sagacity of their ancestors. Greek philosophy and every form of general theory were neglected. The literary language was rude and unfixed; the scanty literature consisted of a few hymns and folk-songs in Saturnian metre, and of such primitive forms of dramatic composition as Fescennine verses, "saturæ" and mimes. Thus eventually, by the last quarter of the third century B.C., the Romans found themselves in control of a vast territory with a population of nearly six millions, from which they could have raised at need no less than 770,000 soldiers, horse and foot: 273,000 citizens, 85,000 Latins, and 412,000 allies.

* * *

In 218 Hannibal descended from the Alps into the Valley of the Po, at the head of the army with which the Carthaginian plutocracy hoped to destroy their upstart rival. To invade a country which could raise 700,000 men at need, with a comparatively small force operating at an immense distance from its base, was a feat of almost incredible daring. But the very fact that the issue remained doubtful for years is clear proof of the inherent weakness of the federation of rural republics that had Rome for its head. Where the mode of life—of feeling and thinking and holding property—is not identical, where, in a word, there is not one definite type of civilisation common at least to the upper and middle classes, there can be no organic nation, but only an accumulation of individuals held together for a time by the discipline of force. Now the agricultural and military aristocracy of ancient Rome had been able to diffuse its civilisation over but a small part of Italy. The dispersion of small Latin proprietors in colonies and *municipia* connected Rome with many regions of Italy by the ties of language, tradition and policy; but the colonies and *municipia* did not at that time cover even one half of the territory of Italy. The rest of the country was in the hands of allied cities, agricultural and aristocratic republics for the most part, which maintained a vigorous local life of their own almost entirely undisturbed by the central power. The Romans had indeed done their best,

especially in Etruria and Southern Italy, to protect the territorial nobility, and had made them the supporters of the Roman cause in the allied cities; they had put an end to their murderous feuds, set them in command of contingents levied among the sturdy race of yeomen, and provided them with the means of winning distinction in war, of increasing both their wealth and their influence among their own countrymen. Thus it happened that the great families of Etruria and Southern Italy were bound by ties of hospitality, friendship, and sometimes even of blood to the foremost houses of Rome; and they were proud of it. They gladly learnt the Latin language and affected an admiration for the great city and its institutions, for the ideas and manners of its nobility. But the people among whom they lived continued each to speak its own national tongue and to keep alive the memories of old days, now wrapped in the halo of an irrevocable past. Possibly Hannibal may have had some inkling of this widespread sentiment; perhaps he dimly understood that Italy was not yet a nation, but a confederation of little States many of which lived their own life by themselves, connected with the central power by only the loosest of bonds. His policy, at any rate, gives colour to the supposition. By promises, stratagems, or threats he persuaded many of the allied cities to revolt, while the Roman citizens and Latin colonists, welded together by the common danger into a true nation of aristocratic peasant-soldiers, heroically defended the land that their fathers had conquered, tilled and peopled, against the champion of the arrogant plutocracy of Carthage.

Rome conquered in the end; for the solid virtues of many generations of mediocrity prevailed over the fortuitous and personal greatness of genius. But the old order, broken down by nearly a generation of fighting, could no more be reconstituted. In the tension of so unprecedented an effort, in the crisis of a war that lasted seventeen years, and not in Italy only, but in Spain, Greece, Sicily and Africa, Rome unlearnt much of her pedantic and superstitious conservatism. She had consumed all her reserves both of public and private wealth, as well as the vast plunder of Syracuse and Carthage; she had improved her military organisation and equipment; she had gained new opportunities for commercial enterprise; and she had relaxed the strictness with which she kept watch over her conduct. The observance of many political traditions, and of a few laws, such as that concerning the age and succession of magistracies, was indefinitely suspended. The old-fashioned prudence made way for a new spirit of adventure, whose typical embodiment was Publius Scipio. Only thus was it possible to bring the great war to a conclusion. Its results seemed a sufficient justification of the policy that produced them—the suzerainty of Spain, and the complete mastery of Sicily: the confiscation of part of the rich territory of Campania and Leontini: the ruin of Capua, and the weakening of all the non-Latinised Italian peoples: the 120,000 pounds of silver that Scipio brought home from Africa, and the annual tribute of 200 talents of silver that was imposed on Carthage for the next half-century.

IV. APPETITE FOR POWER

Theodor Mommsen

THE RELUCTANT TYRANNY

A giant of Germanic scholarship, Theodor Mommsen (1817–1903) was a prolific writer whose bibliography contains some 1,500 items ranging from jurisprudence and German politics to epigraphy and ancient history. His most famous work is *The History of Rome*. Politically active in the nineteenth-century unification of Germany, Mommsen sympathetically idealized Rome's unification of the Mediterranean.

POLYBIUS dates from the battle of Pydna [168 B.C.] the full establishment of the universal empire of Rome. It was in fact the last battle in which a civilized state confronted Rome in the field on a footing of equality with her as a great power; all subsequent struggles were rebellions or wars with peoples beyond the pale of the Romano-Greek civilization —with barbarians, as they were called. The whole civilized world thenceforth recognized in the Roman senate the supreme tribunal, whose commissions decided in the last resort between kings and nations; and to acquire its language and manners foreign princes and youths of quality resided in Rome. A clear and earnest attempt to get rid of this dominion was in reality made only once—by the great Mithradates of Pontus. The battle of Pydna, moreover, marks the last occasion on which the senate still adhered to the state-maxim that they should, if possible, hold no possessions and maintain no garrisons beyond the Italian seas, but should keep the numerous states dependent on them in order by a mere political supremacy. The aim of their policy was that these states should neither decline into utter weakness and anarchy, as had nevertheless happened in Greece nor emerge out of their half-free position into complete independence, as Macedonia had attempted to do not without success. No state was to be allowed utterly to perish, but no one was to be permitted to stand on its own resources. Accordingly the vanquished foe held at least an equal, often a better, position with the Roman diplomatists than the faithful ally; and, while a defeated opponent was reinstated, those who attempted to reinstate themselves were abased—as the Aetolians, Macedonia after the Asiatic war, Rhodes, and Pergamus learned by experience. But not only did this part of protector soon prove as irksome to the masters as to the servants; the Roman protectorate, with its ungrateful Sisyphian toil that continually needed to be begun afresh, showed itself to be intrinsically untenable. Indications of a change of

From *The History of Rome*, translated by William Purdie Dickson (New York, 1908), III, 519–522.

system, and of an increasing disin-
clination on the part of Rome to
tolerate by its side intermediate states
even in such independence as was
possible for them, were very clearly
given in the destruction of the
Macedonian monarchy after the
battle of Pydna. The more and more
frequent and more and more un-
avoidable intervention in the internal
affairs of the petty Greek states
through their misgovernment and
their political and social anarchy; the
disarming of Macedonia, where the
northern frontier at any rate urgently
required a defence different from that
of mere posts; and, lastly, the introduction of the payment of land-tax
to Rome from Macedonia and Illyria,
were so many symptoms of the ap-
proaching conversion of the client
states into subjects of Rome.

If we glance back at the career of
Rome from the union of Italy to the
dismemberment of Macedonia, the
universal empire of Rome, far from
appearing as a gigantic plan contrived
and carried out by an insatiable thirst
for territorial aggrandizement, appears to have been a result which
forced itself on the Roman government without, and even in opposition
to, its wish. It is true that the former
view naturally suggests itself—Sallust
is right when he makes Mithradates
say that the wars of Rome with tribes,
cities, and kings originated in one and
the same prime cause, the insatiable
longing after dominion and riches;
but it is an error to give forth this
judgment—influenced by passion and
the event—as a historical fact. It is
evident to every one whose observation is not superficial, that the Roman
government during this whole period

wished and desired nothing but the
sovereignty of Italy; that they were
simply desirous not to have too powerful neighbours alongside of them; and
that—not out of humanity towards
the vanquished, but from the very
sound view that they ought not to
suffer the kernel of their empire to
be stifled by the shell—they earnestly
opposed the introduction first of
Africa, then of Greece, and lastly of
Asia into the sphere of the Roman
protectorate, till circumstances in
each case compelled, or at least suggested with irresistible force, the extension of that sphere. The Romans
always asserted that they did not pur-
sue a policy of conquest, and that they
were always the party assailed; and
this was something more, at any rate,
than a mere phrase. They were in
fact driven to all their great wars
with the exception of that concerning
Sicily—to those with Hannibal and
Antiochus, no less than to those with
Philip and Perseus—either by a direct
aggression or by an unparalleled dis-
turbance of the existing political
relations; and hence they were ordinarily taken by surprise on their out-
break. That they did not after victory
exhibit the moderation which they
ought to have done in the interest
more especially of Italy itself; that the
retention of Spain, for instance, the
undertaking of the guardianship of
Africa, and above all the half-fanciful
scheme of bringing liberty everywhere
to the Greeks, were in the light of
Italian policy grave errors, is sufficiently clear. But the causes of these
errors were, on the one hand a blind
dread of Carthage, on the other a still
blinder enthusiasm for Hellenic liberty; so little did the Romans exhibit

during this period the lust of conquest, that they, on the contrary, displayed a very judicious dread of it. The policy of Rome throughout was not projected by a single mighty intellect and bequeathed traditionally from generation to generation; it was the policy of a very able but somewhat narrow-minded deliberative assembly, which had far too little power of grand combination, and far too much of a right instinct for the preservation of its own commonwealth, to devise projects in the spirit of a Caesar or a Napoleon. The universal empire of Rome had its ultimate ground in the political development of antiquity in general. The ancient world knew nothing of a balance of power among nations; and therefore every nation which had attained internal unity strove either directly to subdue its neighbours, as did the Hellenic states, or at any rate to render them innocuous, as Rome did,—an effort, it is true, which also issued ultimately in subjugation. Egypt was perhaps the only great power in antiquity which seriously pursued a system of equilibrium: on the opposite system Seleucus and Antigonus, Hannibal and Scipio, came into collision. And, if it seems to us sad that all the other richly-endowed and highly-developed nations of antiquity had to perish in order to enrich a single one out of the whole, and that all in the long run appear to have only arisen to contribute to the greatness of Italy and to the decay involved in that greatness, yet historical justice must acknowledge that this result was not produced by the military superiority of the legion over the phalanx, but was the necessary development of the international relations of antiquity generally—so that the issue was not decided by provoking chance, but was the fulfilment of an unchangeable, and therefore endurable, destiny.

Stringfellow Barr

THE HUNGRY WOLF

The career of Stringfellow Barr (1897–   ), ranging from Professor at the University of Virginia to president of St. John's College in Annapolis, is not restricted to a scholar's ivory tower. For ten years president of the Foundation for World Government, his concern for the problems of today blends well with his interest in antiquity. Among his varied publications, *The Will of Zeus* is perhaps the most literate twentieth-century history of Greece and reflects a humanist's view of the past. In this selection, the noble, virtuous and pious Romans of Livy and Barrow have disappeared and in their place are slaughtering legions. Is this a true contradiction of previous authors? Or are these the same Romans with some characteristics magnified and others suppressed?

ACCORDING to this western republic's own traditions, the mother of Rome's founder was the daughter of a nearby king, whose father dedicated her, while yet a virgin, to a temple. There Mars, god of war, violated her, and she gave birth to twins, Romulus and Remus. Like so many other folk heroes, including Moses and Cyrus the Great, the unwanted baby brothers were exposed. They were placed in some sort of small casket and cast adrift on the Tiber River. But the gods brought them to shore and a she-wolf suckled them. Although the wolf was an animal sacred to Mars, it should be pointed out that the word *lupa*, Latin for she-wolf, was also a word for prostitute, so that maybe the two bastard brothers were suckled, if not borne, by a prostitute. In any event, the two outcasts founded two settlements close together. The one that

Romulus founded, Rome, endured. She welcomed exiles, refugees, and robbers as to a kind of asylum, and together they raided a nearby settlement of Sabines, and kidnapped wives for themselves. Romulus became Rome's first king, and six other kings followed. In the end, Tarquin the Proud, an Etruscan, violated the wife of a noble, whereupon the nobles drove him out and proclaimed a republic, the Res Publica Romana, literally the Roman Public Thing.

But the Greek world told other tales about how Rome had come into being. The Greeks related that some of the adventures of Odysseus had occurred in Italy, and some Greeks claimed that Odysseus had a bastard son by Circe, the witch-goddess with whom Odysseus had lain. This happened at the Circean promontory halfway down the coast from Rome to Naples, where Circe had changed

Odysseus' men into swine. And this son by Odysseus Circe named Romus, and this Romus founded Rome. Still other Greeks sought the origins of Rome, not in the *Odyssey*, but in the *Iliad*. There they read Poseidon's speech to the gods concerning Aeneas. Poseidon predicted that this human son of the goddess Aphrodite would escape the fall of Troy and "be king among the Trojans, and his sons' sons that shall be born in days to come." The Greeks read also how Poseidon saved his life when he was fighting Achilles, as once before Apollo and Aphrodite had saved him. The Greeks concluded that after Troy fell, Aeneas led a band of survivors to Sicily and then to Italy. Perhaps he was the true founder of Capua, the oldest Greek colony in Italy. In any case, he founded Rome. Or a son of his named Romus did. Or a daughter named Rome. This Greek account of Rome as a reborn Troy was widely accepted by the Romans themselves within two or three decades of Alexander's death. Finally, Greeks were capable of assuming that Rome was just another Greek colony, a northern extension of Great Greece, which the Romans called *Magna Graecia.* For instance, according to Plutarch, one of Plato's pupils wrote not long after 390 B.C., when the Gauls sacked Rome, that "out of the West a story prevailed, how an army of Hyperboreans had come from afar and captured a Greek city called Rome, situated somewhere on the shores of the Great Sea."

As history, this medley of often contradictory traditions may have left much to be desired; but as poetic myth it was eloquent of Rome's growing confidence that she could turn obscure origins into proud achievement, appalling defeat into triumphant victory, a human wolf pack into an ordered society; and all because the gods had chosen her. The god-fearing refugee, Aeneas, had taught her, too, to fear the gods; and that those Romans best served the gods who best served the Res Publica, the Public Thing. The Roman Thing had been carved out of this western wilderness by a saving remnant from across the sea. Neither men with ideas, such as the Greeks, nor writers of great tragedies or of unseemly comedies, nor dancers nor musicians nor lyric poets nor philosophizing pedants could have done so much. Neither Greek athletes lolling in shameful nakedness nor the sculptors who loved to make statues of them; neither insolent democrats nor self-seeking aristocrats nor luxury-loving kings could have done it. It could only be done by the sober, severe, modest, disciplined people of the toga. These could be unbreakable in defeat, moderate and just in victory, precisely because they had been chosen by the gods themselves for a manifest destiny. It was their mission to rule more frivolous folk. That they should do so was the will of *Jupiter Optimus Maximus,* Jupiter Greatest and Best. Once handed this commission, and once having bound themselves by relations with him that were contractual, punctilious, and formal, they had set to work. To this labor, therefore, they were bound by their religion. Was not *religio* etymologically a binding together? Was not their word for law, *lex,* also a binding? To accomplish their task, they must acquire power and authority, over themselves and over others. And since their task lay, not in the sky where Jupiter reigned, but here on the south bank of the Tiber, near the west coast of Central Italy, they were determined to deal with the concrete, the practical, the here, the now, and always with things: with men, arms, land, farm tools, seed, flocks, herds, money. Even empty space was a thing, at least in the metaphor. of the poet Ennius, who wrote of "the piled spaces of the ether." The total of what they built or seized would be the Roman Thing, the Res Publica, the Republic. It was this Roman Thing, rather than the invisible gods who had willed it, that they passionately loved. They would love it, defend it, extend it, and die for it. But because their religion bound them to do so, they would do it gravely and with dignity. They would govern it, along with those whom it subjected and bound to itself by solemn treaty and by law. They therefore gave themselves to war, to law, and to labor on this land of theirs.

As to the actual history of the Roman Republic, from the time that Romulus, or Aeneas, or somebody else established *Roma Quadrata,* Foursquare Rome, to the time when Alexander the Great lay dying in Babylon, not much is precisely known. But, legend aside, the history of Rome had much in common with the histories of Athens or Sparta and indeed of the average Greek polis. The Romans, like the Greeks, were herdsmen speaking an Aryan tongue, who had come down from the north in war bands led by chieftain kings and had imposed their language on the agricultural people they settled amongst. The Latin the Roman spoke was distantly kin to the Greek the Hellene spoke. The alphabet the Roman used was adapted from the Greek alphabet, which Rome borrowed from Greek traders or indirectly through her Etruscan neighbors. For these Etruscans, who were commonly thought to have migrated to Italy from Lydia in Asia Minor, had borrowed much from the Greeks they traded with, including the Greek alphabet. The Roman kings consolidated villages into a small city-state. At Rome, as in Greece, the king was chosen by a small class of warriors, who composed his council. In Athens these aristocrats were the Eupatrids, the Well-fathered; in Rome they were the patricians, those citizens who were descended from the *Patres,* or Fathers, who headed their respective clans. The kings whom these nobles chose were formally acclaimed by the humbler members of the polis gathered in a popular assembly. The king was commander-in-chief in time of war, high priest and therefore intermediary between his people and their gods, and the judge who interpreted and applied their laws to the wrongdoer. In Rome as in Greece, settled life brought a shift from monarchy to an aristocratic republic, a shift that was far from reflecting a popular revolt. For example, in Roman tradition, the body of the common people, known as the plebs, looked to Romulus to protect it against the rapacious patricians; the patricians were charged with murdering Romulus; and they could quiet the plebeians only by reporting that Romulus had been whisked up to heaven by the gods. And, just as it was a patrician who murdered the last Roman king, so it was patricians who proclaimed Republican liberty.

In the Roman Republic as in Athens the law was unwritten. In the Athenian republic, only the Eupatrid could interpret the will of Zeus and the lesser gods and enforce it in Athens as human law, just as in Rome only the patrician could interpret the will of Zeus, whom Romans knew as Jupiter, or Jove. In both instances the lower class loudly demanded written law. According to an Athenian saying, Dracon wrote his laws in blood. Similarly harsh law was written at Rome in the Twelve Tables by the Decemvirs, a special commission of ten patricians who for a while ruled the city. In Rome as in Athens, the burning issues were the redistribution of land, or at least the abolition of mortgages; and the scaling down of interest on debts, or the abolition of the creditor's right to imprison or enslave his insolvent debtor. The Twelve Tables, Rome's first written law, even provided that creditors with claims against the same insolvent debtor might carve up his body and divide it among them. The plebeians were so indignant with the continued rule of the Commission of Ten that they seceded from the Res Publica, gathered on the nearby Aventine Mount, constituted a sort of plebeian republic within the Roman Republic, and created new officials called tribunes. The persons of these tribunes were declared inviolable and they were charged with representing the interests of the plebs and with negotiating with the patrician Senate and the two patrician consuls. The consuls were annually elected administrative officers who had replaced the king, just as the annually elected archon had replaced the Athenian king.

The so-called Aventine Secession and the *de facto* establishment of a plebeian legislative chamber occurred about 449, about a century and a half after Athens had given Solon emergency powers to reform her laws and avert a class war. Not even Solon's wise provisions had prevented Pisistratus from setting up a tyranny, a tyranny that did much to rescue the poor of Athens from economic and legal oppression. But another development also helped Athens to create political democracy. The farm land of Attica was not rich, and its poverty steadily urged Athens to take to the sea, to commerce, and to industry.

At the time that the Roman plebs solemnly assembled on the Aventine, Athenian democracy, led by Pericles, was at the height of its glory. It was perhaps not by chance that the Aventine Mount, where the plebs took their Sacred Oath to defend themselves against oppression, was the site of a trading community. Four similar secessions occurred, always to the same site. Among the traders on the Aventine were Greeks, and those Greeks can scarcely have been ignorant of the revolutions that had converted so many Greek cities from aristocracy to democracy. Rome, however, was ill fitted to make that transition. Under the late monarchy she had developed a little local industry, but she did not take to the sea. The pottery she bought from Athenian and Corinthian traders she could pay for in salt from pans at the mouth of the Tiber, timber from upstream, slaves captured in constant wars with her neighbors. The volcanic soil in her valleys was far richer than Attic soil, and her farmers, patrician and plebeian alike, could grow plenty of spelt, a species of wheat admittedly better suited to making porridge than to making bread. In the nearby hills Rome had good pasture for cattle. Finally, throughout the fifth and a part of the fourth centuries, her constant wars with her neighbors tended to cut her off from intercourse with the world beyond and from any large-scale exchange either of commodities or of ideas.

For these reasons Rome turned in on herself, as Sparta had done somewhat earlier. Like Sparta, she was oligarchical in politics, inland and not maritime, proud of her simple living, not much given to art, unfriendly to speculation, harsh of wit, grave of manner. But she was unlike Sparta too: no legendary laws of Lycurgus forbade her governing class to own land privately or to amass what money they could get hold of. And though her poorer peasants were cruelly ground down, they were not state serfs like the Spartan Helots, shut out entirely from the political community. Moreover, while the Spartan spent his whole life in training for war and abstained from labor, the Roman patrician of the early Republic was proud to farm with his own hands. Sparta strove to exercise the hegemony of the Peloponnese. But once she had acquired neighboring Messenia, she tried to hold hegemony by maintaining a highly trained standing army rather than by wars of conquest, if only because of the specter of an uprising of Helots at

home. Rome, however, managed to be at war almost constantly and to make war pay: in booty, in money indemnity, in land, and in allied manpower available for the next struggle.

* * *

When Rome's long struggle with her neighbors had apparently ended in her favor, the Greek world of Alexander sent the Italian peninsula not wisdom or philosophic inquiry but force. About 338, some two years before Alexander succeeded Philip as King of Macedon, Tarentum, a Greek port inside the heel of Italy, called in a Spartan king to defend it against the hill tribes of Lucania, but he was defeated. A few years later Tarentum appealed to Alexander, King of Epirus, uncle and brother-in-law of Alexander of Macedon, then warring in Asia. Alexander of Epirus crossed the Adriatic with an army, fought the hill tribes, and also gained control of most of Magna Graecia. But Tarentum came to distrust its rescuer, and in the end he was killed by Lucanians. A third appeal brought over Cleonymus, son of a Spartan king, with a third army of mercenaries, but the Tarentines soon quarreled with him and he returned to Greece.

Rome, too, had been drawn into the affairs of Magna Graecia. Capua and other Greek cities in Campania sought and obtained a Roman alliance against the predatory mountain tribes of Samnium, in the southern Apennines. This of course embroiled Rome with the Samnites, who had previously helped her against the Gauls. In 321, two years after Alex-

ander the Great died in Babylon, a
Roman army of 20,000 men was
trapped by the Samnites in the Cau-
dine Forks, a defile in the southern
Apennines, and was forced to surrender. But by now Rome and her
Latin Allies could draw on a free
population of probably 750,000: she
increased her levies and raised her
field army to between 35,000 and
40,000 men. She also borrowed from
Samnite tactics.

In the third century, the Academy
Plato had founded and the Lyceum
Aristotle had established still flour-
ished in Athens but found a rival, the
Museum, which Ptolemy I set up in
Alexandria for teaching, research,
and literary work. The Museum became the center for the extraordinary
flowering of mathematics and natural science that made the third
century the great period of the Hellenistic intellect. Rome spent this
third century fighting seven wars,
which covered about seventy years.
The first of these struggles was the
Third Samnite War, ending in 290.

In 281 Tarentum, fearing Rome's
intrusions into the affairs of Magna
Graecia, called in another king of
Epirus, named Pyrrhus, with 25,000
men. In the Hellenistic world he was
generally considered the ablest commander of his day. Pyrrhus met a
Roman army at Heraclea. His phalanx of pikemen could do nothing
against the Roman infantry, whose
tactics were more flexible and who
were already celebrated for "persever-
ance and endurance." But the horses
of Rome's cavalry were terrified by
his elephants, and Pyrrhus outflanked
the Roman infantry and won his
battle. The Romans showed no sign

of discouragement, and Pyrrhus sent
an envoy to Rome to try negotiation.
According to later tradition, this envoy reported that

The senate impressed him as a council
of many kings, and that, as for the people, he was afraid it might prove to be a
Lernaean hydra for them to fight
against, since the consul already had
twice as many soldiers collected as those
who faced their enemies before, and
there were many times as many Romans
still who were capable of bearing arms.

At Asculum, a year later, the elephants nearly won for Pyrrhus again,
but the Roman infantry fell back on
their fortified camp. Magna Graecia
had gone over to him; so had the
Lucanians and the Samnites. He
marched into Latium, got within fifty
miles of Rome, and tried to detach
Rome's Latin allies, but to no avail.
He proved he could outgeneral Rome,
but it did him no good. His losses were
heavy, Rome's manpower was indeed a hydra, and, when some of the
Greek cities of Sicily invited Pyrrhus
over to help them drive out of the
island their centuries-old enemies,
the Carthaginians, Pyrrhus promptly
sought glory in Sicily. When, however, the Greeks there began to quarrel with him and when his allies in
Magna Graecia, now hard pressed by
Rome, begged him to return, he left
for Italy again. There the Roman
army made the interesting discovery
that elephants, if wounded by jave-
lins, had a way of losing their heads
and trampling their own army. When
at last it became apparent that
Pyrrhus could liberate neither Greek
Sicily from Carthage nor Magna
Graecia from Rome, he salvaged
eight thousand of his infantry and

five hundred horse, went home to
Epirus, recruited some Gallic mercenaries, and attacked Macedonia. After
many adventures he met his death in
272 in a street battle in Argos.

Eight years later, Rome had again
subjected all of Magna Graecia. She
now controlled the whole of Italy
south of the Po Valley, which she still
called Cisalpine Gaul, or Gaul this
side of the Alps. Pyrrhus had won
many victories over her troops, but
they had all turned out to be Pyrrhic
victories. He was the last of the four
military adventurers who had led their
mercenaries out of Alexander's Hellenistic Cosmopolis to liberate the
Western Greeks, in Magna Graecia
or in Sicily, from neighboring tribes,
from Carthage, or from Rome. It was
symbolic of Rome's success that the
year before Pyrrhus was killed in Argos, King Ptolemy of Egypt, one of the
three most powerful states in Cosmopolis, entered into a treaty of
friendship with the Roman Republic.
The Roman Public Thing had constructed a network of alliances with
all the cities and tribes of peninsular
Italy, alliances which guaranteed
Rome money-tribute from many of
them and immense military man-
power. Many of them had been forced
also to surrender land, on which Rome
planted military colonies. Those colonies answered two purposes: they
made it risky for Rome's allies to
revolt against her control, and they
helped to satisfy the land hunger of
her own growing population. The
same two objects had been served in
the fifth century by the cleruchies,
or military colonies, of imperial
Athens.

* * *

The long years of war that gave the
Roman Republic control over peninsular Italy and that witnessed four
armed interventions launched from
the Hellenistic world gave Rome the
appearance of having remained what
the Romulus legends declared her: a
city of outlaws and robbers suckled
by a she-wolf, a city of lovers of
violence. But that appearance was de-
ceptive in one respect. Certainly any
Greek who was fond of etymology
might be pardoned for noting that the
Greek transliteration of *Roma*, Rome,
happened conveniently to be a Greek
word for violence. Certainly the temple of the god Janus, which was
opened only when the Republic was
at war, had, according to tradition,
never been closed but once. Certainly
violence played an enormous role in
Rome's history: though she won some
of peninsular Italy by diplomacy, she
won most of it by the sword. Within
the city the relation of patrician to
plebeian was one of tension, often one
of brutal oppression tempered by last-
minute compromise. As for the relation between free man and slave, this,
as in democratic Athens, was necessarily a relation of force, and the Roman was a more brutal master if only
because he had perhaps less imagination than the Athenian. Witnesses to
that brutality are the successive slave
revolts that Rome put down, in 501, in
499, in 498; whereas before the Roman conquest Athens seems to have
experienced none, except at the Su-
nium silver mines during the Pelo-
ponnesian War. In 419 bands of
slaves marched on Rome in an unsuc-

cessful effort to burn it. Moreover, at various times Rome's allies tried in vain to throw off her control. In the allied cities the populace would often have preferred independence, if Roman armies had not been available to the Roman patriciate to maintain local oligarchies like itself in power.

In short, the City of the She-Wolf controlled peninsular Italy largely by organized violence. On the other hand, the violence of intruders from the Hellenistic world, such as Pyrrhus, tended to be aimless, even if its declared purpose was to liberate the Western Greeks from barbarous neighbors, from Carthage, from Rome. The She-Wolf's depredations did bring order. She protected the cities of Italy, whether Latin, Italic, or Greek, from pillaging mountain tribes; Etruria, from the Cisalpine Gauls. She protected the cities from each other. In each city she protected men of substance from revolution. She charged a good commission, in the form of military support, for her services, whether or not she fixed the rate too high. She pacified Italy at a time when the Hellenistic world was still torn by war, both foreign and civil. Whether or not Jove really commissioned the Roman people to rule, they were rapidly on the way to becoming "the strongest" people in the whole Mediterranean basin, and thereby to claiming Alexander's Cosmopolis.

Montesquieu

TREACHEROUS ENCROACHMENT

Born to a life of aristocratic indolence, Charles Louis de Secondat, Baron de la Brède et de Montesquieu (1689–1755) devoted much of his energy to writing with wit. *The Spirit of the Laws* helped provide a philosophic base for the American Revolution. *The Greatness and Decline of Rome* coolly analyzed the moral tone and strategic factors in the growth, consolidation and decline of Rome's rule over the Mediterranean, from the viewpoint of one enjoying Machiavellian politics. Is Montesquieu seeing the Romans through the eye of Machiavelli, or is he illustrating Machiavelli by using the Romans?

IN the course of their good fortune, which usually makes men negligent, the Roman Senate always acted with the same profundity. While their armies were dismaying all others, the Senate held down the defeated.

The Senate set up a tribunal which judged all peoples. At the end of every war, it decided the penalties and rewards which each deserved. It took a part of the land of the conquered to give to the allies, so accomplishing two things: it attached to Rome kings from which it had little to fear and much to hope, and it weakened others, from whom it had nothing to hope and much to fear.

Allies were used to make war on an enemy, but the victors were immediately destroyed. Philip was conquered by the Aetolians, who were annihilated immediately afterward for joining with Antiochus. Antiochus was conquered with the help of the Rhodians; but after the Rhodians were given surprising rewards, they were humbled forever, on the pretext that they tried to make peace with Perseus.

When the Romans had several enemies at hand, they made a treaty with the weakest, who felt lucky to get it, glad to have postponed their ruin.

As soon as they were involved in a major war, the Senate ignored all sorts of insults and waited in silence for the time of punishment to come. If the people sent the guilty ones, the Senate refused to punish them, preferring to consider all the nation criminal and to reserve it for a useful vengeance.

Since the Romans made inconceivable hardships for their enemies, no league was made against them, for those who were farthest away from danger scarcely wished to come closer to it.

They rarely entered into war, but always made it in the time, in the way, and against whom they chose. Of the many peoples they attacked, there were few who would not have put up

From Montesquieu, *Considerations sur les Causes de la Grandeur des Romains* (Paris: Editions Garnier Frères, 1954), pp. 31–40. Translated by the editor.

with all sorts of insults, if Rome had been willing to leave them in peace.

Their custom was always to speak as masters, so the ambassadors the Romans sent to the peoples who had not yet felt their power were certainly maltreated, which was a pretext for making a new war.

Since they never made peace in good faith, and since their plan was to invade everywhere, their treaties were actually only suspensions of war, and they always put in conditions which began the ruin of the state that accepted their terms. They forbade garrisons in strong places, or restricted the number of land troops, or demanded the surrender of horses or elephants. If the nation was a sea power, they made it burn its ships and sometimes made the people live farther inland.

After destroying the armies of a king, they ruined his economy by excessive taxes or a tribute, under pretext of having him pay the war costs; this was a new form of tyranny which forced him to oppress his subjects and so lose their love.

As soon as they settled a peace with a ruler, they took one of his brothers or sons as a hostage. This gave them the means to disturb the realm at their whim. When they had the immediate heir, they intimidated the incumbent; if they had only a distantly related prince, they used him to stir up popular revolts.

When a prince or a people revolted against the authority of their sovereign, the Romans immediately accorded them the title of Ally of the Roman People, thus making them sacred and inviolable. There was no king, however great he might be, who could be sure of his subjects or even his family.

Although the title of Ally was a sort of servitude, it was nevertheless much sought after. The Romans made sure that their allies were only insulted by them. An Ally could hope that these insults would be less than otherwise. Thus, there was no service that some peoples and kings were not ready to give, and no lengths to which they would not go to obtain this title.

The Romans had all sorts of allies. Some were tied to them by privileges and a share of Roman grandeur, like the Latins and the Hernicii; others, from the time of their settlement, like their colonies; some by benefits, as were Massinissa, Eumenes and Attalus, who held from the Romans their realm or their advancement; others by free treaties, and these became subjects by a long custom of alliance, like the kings of Egypt, of Bithynia, of Cappadocia, and most of the Greek cities; several more by forced treaties and by the terms of their submission, like Philip and Antiochus. The Romans made no peace with an enemy without terms of alliance, subjecting only people who served them to humble others.

When they left some cities in freedom, they immediately caused two factions to rise there. One defended the laws and liberty of the country, the other maintained that there was no law but the will of the Romans. Since the latter faction was always the more powerful, it is obvious that such a freedom was only in name.

Sometimes they made themselves masters of a country under pretext of succession. They entered into Asia, Bithynia and Lybia by the wills of Attalus, Nicomedes and Appius; Egypt was captured by the will of the king of Cyrene.

To keep great rulers weak, they did not want them to make alliances with those leagued with Rome. Since the Romans refused alliance to no neighbor of a powerful ruler, this condition in a peace treaty left the ruler with no allies.

Further, having vanquished some important ruler, they put in the treaty that he was not to make war over any quarrels with allies of the Romans (usually including all his neighbors), but that he was to submit the quarrels for arbitration. This left him no future in military power.

Further, to keep all power for themselves, the Romans even took it away from their allies. As soon as these began to quarrel, the Romans sent ambassadors who made them make peace. See how they ended the wars of Attalus and Prusias.

When some ruler had made a conquest, which had often exhausted his resources, a Roman ambassador would immediately appear to seize it from his hands. Among a thousand examples one might recall how, with a word, they chased Antiochus from Egypt.

Knowing how adept the peoples of Europe were in war, the Romans established as a law that it was not permitted for any Asian king to enter Europe and there subjugate any people. The main grounds for the war against Mithridates was that, breaking this rule, he had subjugated some barbarians.

If they saw two peoples at war, although they might have not the slightest alliance nor concern with either party, they never failed to appear on the scene, and, like knights in shining armor, they took the part of the weakest. It was, says Dionysius of Halicarnassus, an old custom of the Romans always to give their help to anyone who asked it.

These customs of the Romans were not chance incidents; they were regular principles. The maxims which they used against the greatest powers were exactly those which they had used from the beginning against the little towns around them.

They used Eumenes and Massinissa to subjugate Philip and Antiochus, as they had used the Latins and Hernicii to subjugate the Volscians and the Tuscans. They had taken the fleets of Carthage and the Asian kings as they had taken the ships of Antium. They forbade political and civil liaisons among the four parts of Macedonia, as they had formerly broken the union of the little Latin cities.

But above all, their constant maxim was to divide. The republic of Achaea was formed by an association of free cities. The Senate declared that each city should govern itself henceforth by its own laws, without depending on a common authority.

The republic of Boeotia was similarly a league of several towns; when, in the war against Perseus, some sided with Perseus and the others with the Romans, they took the latter party into favor to dissolve the Boeotian alliance.

If a great prince[1] ruling in our times had followed these maxims,

[1] Montesquieu is probably referring to Louis XIV. [Editor's note.]

when he saw one of his neighbors dethroned, the prince would have used overwhelming force to help and support the neighbor in the part of the nation which remained true to him. By dividing the only power which could oppose his plans, he would have received immense advantage from the misfortunes of his ally.

When there were disputes within a state, the Romans would immediately judge the matter, and so they would be sure to be opposed only by the party they condemned. If rulers of the same blood argued over a crown, the Romans sometimes declared them co-rulers. If one of them was under age, they decided in his favor, and took him in tutelage, as protectors of all the world. Things reached the point that both the peoples and the kings were their subjects, without precisely being known by that title, since the Romans insisted that it was enough to have heard of them to become subordinate to them.

They never made distant wars without having secured some ally near the enemy they attacked who could join his troops to the army they sent. Since that army was never large in number, they were always careful to keep another in the province nearest to the enemy, and a third in Rome always ready to march. Thus they exposed only a small part of their forces, while their enemy risked all of his.

Sometimes they abused the subtlety of the terms of their language. They destroyed Carthage, saying that they had promised to preserve the population and not the city. We know how the Aetolians, who had surrendered in good faith, were deceived: the Romans claimed that the meaning of the words "to surrender in good faith to an enemy" meant the loss of all sorts of things—of people, lands, cities, temples, and even of tombs.

They could even give a treaty an arbitrary new interpretation. Thus, when they wanted to humble the Rhodians, they said that they had not formerly given them Lycia as a present, but as an ally and friend.

When one of their generals made peace to save the army he was about to lose, the Senate would not ratify the peace, but profited from it and continued the war. So, when Jugurtha had surrounded a Roman army and let it go under faith in a Roman treaty, the Romans used the very troops he had saved against him; and when the Numantines had made twenty thousand starving Romans seek a peace, that peace which had saved so many citizens was broken in Rome. The Senate escaped public disapproval by sending the Numantines the Consul who had signed the agreement.

Sometimes they made a private treaty with a ruler under reasonable conditions, but when he had met these, they added others which made him begin the war anew. So, when they had made Jugurtha give up his elephants, horses, treasures, and Roman deserters, they demanded that he give himself up. Since this was the final misfortune for any ruler, it could never be a condition of peace.

Finally, they judged kings for their faults and their crimes. They listened to the complaints of all those who had a quarrel with Philip and sent deputies to protect the complainants. They had Perseus before them accused of murders and quarrels with citizens of allied cities.

Since they rated the glory of a general by the quantity of gold and silver carried in his triumphal parade, they left nothing to the vanquished enemy. Rome was always enriched, and every war put it in condition to undertake another.

The peoples who were friends or allies were all ruined by the immense presents they gave to keep favor or to get more favor. Even half of the money sent to the Romans in this way would have been enough to conquer them.

Masters of the universe, they claimed all its treasures for themselves. They were less unjust as conquerors then as legislators. Knowing that Ptolemy, king of Cyprus, had immense riches, they made a law on the suggestion of a tribune in which they gave themselves the right to inherit from a living man and to confiscate property from an allied prince.

Soon certain greedy men managed to steal that which had escaped the public greed. The magistrates and the governors sold unfair verdicts to kings. (Two competitors would ruin themselves to buy a shaky protection from a rival who had not spent everything. For they had not even that justice of bandits, who keep up a certain honesty in their exercise of crime.) Legitimate or usurped rights were maintained only by money, so the rulers ruined the temples and confiscated the goods of the richest citizens. They committed a thousand crimes to give the Romans all the money in the world.

Notice the conduct of the Romans. After the defeat of Antiochus, they were the masters of Africa, Asia and Greece, with scarcely any cities there of their own. It seemed that they only conquered to give. Yet they remained so much the masters that when they made war on some ruler they crushed him, one might say, under the weight of all the world.

It was not yet time to take over the conquered lands. If they had kept the cities taken from Philip, they would have opened the eyes of the Greeks. If, after the Second Punic War or that against Antiochus, they had taken lands in Africa or in Asia, they could not have kept conquests so weakly established.

They had to wait for all the nations to be used to obeying as free men and allies, before commanding them as subjects, and for them to lose themselves little by little in the Roman Republic.

See the treaty they made with the Latins after the victory of Lake Regulus. It was one of the main bases of their power. Not a single word is there which could arouse suspicions of the empire.

It was a slow way of conquering. They conquered a people and were content to weaken it. They imposed on it conditions which insensibly diminished it. If it rose up, they humbled it still further. Finally it became a subject without anyone being able to name the time of subjugation.

Thus Rome was not strictly a monarchy nor a Republic, but rather the head of a body formed by all the peoples of the world.

It is the folly of conquerors to wish

to give all peoples their laws and customs. That is good for nothing, for people can obey any sort of government.

But Rome imposed no general laws, and the peoples made no dangerous liaisons among themselves. They made a common body only by a common obedience. Without being citizens, they were all Romans.

V. A MODERN SYNTHESIS

Leon Homo

ELEMENTS OF IMPERIALISM

The French historian Leon Homo (1872–1957) taught at the University of Lyons from 1912 to 1940. Although most of his works concentrate on the Roman Empire, the city of Rome and the influence of Christianity on pagan ideals, Professor Homo displays keen insight and lucidity in *Primitive Italy and the Beginnings of Roman Imperialism,* from which this selection is taken.

Which preceding views are combined by Homo in this account? Which are omitted or disregarded? Does he add any new perspectives to the question? Is his balance of factors convincing? Can a final solution to the problem be found?

THE expansion of Roman power beyond Italy from the third century B.C. and the gradual conquest of the Mediterranean basin are facts of history. But was there such a thing as Roman imperialism, and, if so, what were its underlying principles, and how ought its birth and successive stages of growth to be conceived? A throng of theorists, eager to justify the past or even to foretell it, press upon us and deafen us with their discordant clamour. Some propound a theory of deliberate conquest; Rome cold-bloodedly plans the subjugation of the world and methodically realizes her ambitious projects in the teeth of storms and tempests. Others are more sentimental and invoke philhellenism, which would reach its zenith in the proclamation of the Isthmian Games and find its natural corollaries in the war with Antiochus and the Roman intervention in Asia Minor. Others advocate a theory of defensive imperialism; Rome only attacked in self-defence, and it was in spite of herself that she ended by extending her sway over the whole Mediterranean world. Such is the theory, let us examine the main arguments adduced in support of it.

Rome, threatened by neighbouring peoples like the Etruscans, Volscii, and Sabellians, had to subdue them in order to secure peace in Latium. Menaced by invasions of Celts she was forced to assume the leadership of the Italians to ward off the invader, and the conquest of Gaul by Julius Cæsar was itself only the last episode in this long war. The war with Pyrrhus would be defensive and necessary to the achievement of Italian unity. The war with the Semites of Africa would again be defensive; for they represented a first way of Mohammedanism before Mohammed, and their religious fanaticism and mercantile cupidity threatened to

From Leon Homo, *Primitive Italy and the Beginnings of Roman Imperialism* (London, 1927), 253–264, by permission of Routledge and Kegan Paul, Ltd.

overwhelm Italy, and all Europe after her. So, too, with the war against the pirates of Illyria, which was indispensable to secure freedom of trade and the safety of the Adriatic coasts. The war with Hannibal was defensive as a war for territorial integrity and national independence. Similarly with the wars in Spain and Greece, the natural corollaries of the Punic Wars, and attributable, like the latter, to Carthaginian imperialism. Finally, the wars in the East would be defensive, for they resulted from the aggressive policy of Philip and Antiochus, and were acts of self-preservation forced upon unified Italy. No doubt there was a Roman imperialism—it would be thankless to deny it—but at least in its intentions this imperialism had always remained strictly defensive.

Then we are offered a theory of Machiavellianism; for the attainment of her programme Rome displayed a diplomatic astuteness and a political foresight such as mankind has never known before or since. Again, there is the theory of contingence; Roman policy was passive and always followed events; Roman conquest was the result of pure chance explicable by the mere interplay of circumstances; and, in a word, everything in the world conspired to further Roman greatness save the Romans themselves. The list might be continued by the theory of militarist imperialism, the theory of economic imperialism, and a host of others.

To orientate ourselves in this maze of theories, as many as varied, it may be helpful to lay down a few primary truths as stepping-stones. Consider first the geographical factor. Through

her situation in the centre of the Mediterranean basin, with her double coastal frontage on the Tyrrhenian and Adriatic Seas facing west and east, Italy seemed destined by Nature herself to play a dominant part in the history of the Mediterranean. Though this is an indisputable fact, it must not be exaggerated. It was merely a promising possibility which the human factor might or might not transform into a reality. The human factor was in this case, firstly, general circumstances, and, secondly, the temperament of the people fated to exploit these. Rome appeared at her predestined hour between the Oriental world already on the steep slope to decadence and the Western world still sunk in barbarism. The first of all the great Mediterranean countries to transcend the limits of the City-State, Rome had been able to create in a stable form a national unity of a larger type. The Balkan unity, momentarily established by Macedonia, had preceded that of Italy by more than a century in the form of the League of Corinth (338–37), but it had remained incomplete, and, worse still, it had not lasted despite all subsequent attempts at its resurrection. Through this accident, the field was left open to Rome and Italy. As for the Roman people themselves they will remain what we have found them in the hour of the conquest of Italy. Let us not picture the Roman as a stupid boor nor as a superman. His character was dominated by two traits —practical common-sense and lack of imagination. The Roman had no subtle and far-reaching programme of foreign policy. When he was thinking of the future, he did not look beyond the morrow. He did not care to burden his mind with a mass of possibilities the majority of which would never become realities. As a practical man he did not bother about sentiment. His policy was governed by his interests and was realistic, aiming at specific ends near at hand. In these circumstances it is natural that foreign policy appeared primarily as a series of defensive problems.

In 264 B.C. Rome intervened in Sicily and thus gave the signal for the Punic Wars; she did so under the impression of a danger from Carthage:

"The Romans," says Polybius, "beheld the Carthaginians already masters of Africa, of a great part of Spain, and of all the islands washed by the Tyrrhenian and Sardinian Seas. If the same people seized Sicily it was to be feared that they would be extremely inconvenient and formidable neighbours who were encircling Rome and threatening all the coasts of Italy. Now, it was obvious that they would quickly subdue Sicily unless help were given to the Mamertines; for with Messana in their hands they would not take long to capture Syracuse, their sway being already established in almost the whole of Sicily. That is what was foreseen at Rome when it was found necessary not to abandon Messana nor to allow the Carthaginians to use it as a bridge for reaching Italy."

The memory of the great Syracusan tyrants and their policy of active interference in the affairs of the peninsula was too vivid at Rome for men to remain blind to a similar menace. It was just the same in 201 B.C., when the Senate embarked upon the second war with Macedonia, which drew Rome on step by step to the conquest of the whole East. After the first defeat of Carthage and the satisfactory settlement of the Tyrrhenian question, it was generally believed at Rome that Italy was henceforth inviolable, and this feeling soon became a dogma. Hannibal's invasion came as a rude shock and had brusquely opened men's eyes. Hence, peculiarly quick as the Romans were to profit by the lessons of experience, the possibility of a similar danger, coming this time from the east and originating in Macedonia, had soon alarmed public opinion. The Senate, with its coolness and wider information, did not perhaps share these fears, but there was a real danger nearer home, and therefore more serious, which it had resolved to eliminate one day. The Balkan peninsula was at least as populous as Italy. If united it could put as many soldiers into the field. For the sake of Italy's greatness—nay, for her very safety—it was essential to prevent at all costs the revival of that Balkan unity once created momentarily by Philip and Alexander, with new guarantees for stability and permanence. It might seem premature, but it was really prudent to intervene before Macedonia had been able to realize her designs.

The same anxiety for defence was the dominant note at the time of the war with Antiochus. Rome, who had ruined Macedonia's plans upon Greece, did not intend that a new military power should get a footing in the Balkans. To deliver Italy from such a possibility, she did not hesitate to cross over to Asia and cut the wings of the Seleucids' European ambitions by the treaty of 188. Finally, seeing herself threatened sooner or later with revenge by Macedon, she uprooted the evil by suppressing Macedon herself through the war with Perses.

In the history of all great military

powers, it is certain that the intercon-
nection of events has always played a
prominent part. Every victorious campaign paves the way for another
through its consequences and reper-
cussions, and the conquering State
finds herself led on to further conquests, be it only for defensive considerations. Rome was no exception to
the general rule. But, at least in her
case, though the theory of defensive
imperialism explains much, it does
not explain everything. In that long
concatenation of interventions and
conquests there were decisive mo-
ments when Rome had to decide and
the offensive depended on her and on
her alone. Three such cases deserve
attention—the beginning of the Punic
Wars in 264 B.C., the declaration of
war upon Macedon in 200, and the
final conflict with Carthage in the
middle of the second century. Apart
from any theories, however attractive,
what was the attitude of the Roman
Government in these concrete cases?
If we wish to follow through all its
phases the genesis of the idea of conquest at Rome some details are here
necessary.

In 264 B.C., with Pyrrhus out of the
way, Carthage threatened to sub-
merge all Sicily. Syracuse was decadent and could not stop her. Carthaginian forces had been smuggled into
the citadel of Messana by a trick. No
doubt this advance was a threat to the
young unity of Italy, and Polybius, as
we have seen, says so explicitly. But
defensive measures might have sufficed. As for the danger of a Carthaginian invasion of Italy, if it is remembered that, after two centuries of
fierce fighting, she had not succeeded

in conquering the whole of Sicily, we
are justified in remaining sceptical
about such a possibility. In deciding
to assist the Mamertines, Rome deliberately adopted an offensive policy,
whatever her reasons or her pretexts.
On the day when the legions crossed
the Strait of Messina, Roman imperialism, whether wittingly or not, in-
augurated the long series of colonial
wars and launched out upon the conquest of the Mediterranean world.

In 200 B.C., a year after the treaty
of peace ending the Second Punic
War, the Roman Senate placed upon
the agenda for the comitia the question of the declaration of war upon
Macedonia. It knew from experience
that one day the Adriatic question
would provoke a conflict between the
two powers, and the alliance between
the King of Macedonia, Philip V, and
the Seleucid Antiochus III concluded
two years previously had only aggravated her fears. From the standpoint
of defence, however, there was no ur-
gency, and Rome, behind her network
of outposts in Illyria, had time for
thought. Nevertheless, the Senate took
the first step. Politically and mili-
tarily the moment was particularly
propitious. Antiochus was detained in
Asia by his conflict with Egypt, and
his hands were therefore tied. On the
other hand, schooled by the stern
trials of the Second Punic War, the
Roman army was in exceptionally
good condition, such as might never
recur. Throughout the eighteen years
of the war with Hannibal the whole of
Italy had been kept in a continual
state of mobilization, and her citizen
army had thus acquired the value of
a professional machine. Moreover,

there had always been one particularly weak point in the Roman organization—the high command suffered both from incompetence and instability. Now, thanks to the long Punic Wars, both these chronic vices had been, if not permanently eliminated, at least temporarily alleviated. The superior officers had had leisure to train themselves in the field; Scipio Africanus and Flamininus, the future victors of Zama and Cynoscephalæ, who were military tribunes at twenty, had served their apprenticeship to large-scale warfare on the battle-fields of Italy, and in this trial had prepared the triumphs of the future. And so the Senate, fully conscious of the advantages of the moment, chose to settle the Macedonian affair on the spot and acted accordingly.

Finally, it was the same on the eve of the Third Punic War. Rome cold-bloodedly passed the sentence of death on Carthage; her decision was largely influenced by the possibility of the capture of the town by Massinissa, a grave danger for the future which Rome meant to eliminate once for all. On that day she took the initiative and the offensive was due to her, whatever motives she might invoke.

But we, too, are acquainted with this theory whereby war with your neighbour is in the long run inevitable, and which recommends forestalling him as soon as you have—or think you have—all the trumps in your hand. It is just the theory of preventive war, the pet child of all imperialisms, and we know from experience that all lovers of conquest at all times and in all places have always had a weakness for it. According to it

you label preventive the war with Carthage in 264, that with Macedonia in 200, that with Perses in 171, and that with Carthage in 149. That Rome had aimed at the conquest of the world from the end of the third century is, of course, a theory due to oversimplification and merely childish, *pace* Bossuet. No doubt even on the morrow of the defeat of Carthage in 201, the Roman Government had not resolved upon a policy of conquest nor annexation. Admit that considerations of defence always occupied the first place in her deliberations: after all, it remains none the less true that a logical concatenation of events led Rome from the unification of Italy to the conception of an ever-expanding Mediterranean programme and that, with the assistance of the system of preventive war, the ultimate outcome of this programme must mean in the long run the subjugation of the whole Mediterranean world.

The Senate, the organ of Roman foreign policy invested with the powers of a veritable dictatorship since the Second Punic War, bears the main responsibility. No doubt is possible upon this point. The declaration of war upon Macedonia in 201 B.C. had been almost unanimously rejected by the centuries.

"The citizens," says Livy, "were tired after such a long and disastrous war (the Second Punic War), and weariness of dangers and fatigue had naturally impelled them to this refusal. Moreover, the tribune of the plebs, Q. Bæbius, reviving the old practice of recriminations against the senators, accused them of stirring up war after war to prevent the people ever tasting the fruits of peace."

The Senate insisted, had the question restored to the agenda for the comitia, and finally secured a favourable vote. Again in 171 and 149 the Senate, and it alone, took the initiative in the rupture with Perses and then with Carthage. But the people also had its share, a very considerable share, in the responsibility for the direction of Roman foreign policy. As a rule, from the third century onwards it allied itself fully to the Senatorial policy, although less through a true appreciation of the international position as through a care for its own economic interests. A reduction of the capital tax or even its practical remission (from 167), a low cost of living through the reduction of the price of grain, distributions and largesses and fêtes, and spectacles of all kinds were the principal advantages which the populace saw in conquest. And so, apart from its quite passing fit of illtemper in 200, the people ratified the Senate's proposals without a murmur —for instance, in 191 and 171 at the time of the declaration of war with Antiochus and with Perses. Sometimes even it exhibited greater intransigeance than the Senate itself. The First Punic War offers two good illustrations of this attitude. In 264 B.C. the Senate hesitated to accede to the appeal of the Mamertines, it deliberated long without coming to any decision.

"But the people, ruined by the previous wars and ready to jump at any sort of opportunity for repairing its losses and at the same time swayed by the considerations of public interest and the substantial advantages which the consuls held forth to each individual, declared for the expedition. By the decision of the people one of the two consuls, Appius Claudius, was placed in command of a relieving army and was ordered to cross the straits to help Messana."

At the end of the war in 241 B.C., it was the people and not the Senate who rejected as unsatisfactory the provisional terms negotiated by Lutatius Catulus. A commission of ten senators dispatched at their instigation modified and aggravated the terms. Imperialism crowned with victory was beginning to get a hold on the public mind.

The Second Punic War, the sternest trial that Rome had yet endured, marks the critical moment in the formation of Roman imperialism. After fighting for eighteen years for their very lives, Rome and Italy have ended by winning a complete victory. The power of Carthage is broken and nothing in the West can resist them. In the East, on the other hand, the great Hellenistic Oriental monarchies are still intact. The phalanx, the enigma of the moment, still retains its enormous prestige unimpaired, and in the Greek world many still believe in the dogma of its invincibility. The day of Cynoscephalæ dispelled that last illusion, not only in the eyes of the Greeks, but also of the Romans, which was more important.

After her victory over Carthage and Macedon, the two first military powers in the Mediterranean, Rome knew —for a double test had taught her— that henceforth she was all-powerful through her army. From the ability to the will is a short step, and it was soon taken, since imperialism had not received her due. National intoxication and the dizziness of greatness, but also more prosaic and material considerations, as the study of the economic factor will shortly show, swept Rome along the path. Statesmen—I will not say parties, for at this period there were none left—might squabble over domestic policy; in the domain of foreign policy they were agreed. The Scipios, who for the first fifteen years of the second century exercised a predominant influence, and their implacable enemy Cato, worked hand in hand when Rome's greatness was at stake. The idea of imperialism gripped the whole city; in this unanimity the secret of its power and the irresistible force of its expansion are to be found.

And here a serious question arises: How far did the economic factor contribute side by side with the political causes to the formation and growth of Roman imperialism? We shall shortly see its rôle in the middle of the second century B.C., but to what extent did it influence Roman policy during the first half of that century? On this point two conflicting theses are advanced. To some, Roman imperialism was governed primarily by mercantile aims throughout this period. First the great campaigns in the East, and then the simultaneous destruction of Carthage and Corinth, played into the hands of the Roman merchant and speculator. According to others, imperialism at Rome was strictly military in form and was affected by economic considerations either not at all or to a negligible degree. Which party is right? We answer, neither; both theses are too rigid and fail to take into account the natural complexity of the problem and the historical evolution by which it had been conditioned.

No doubt, both through the environment in which it was born and the conditions which had governed its early growth, Roman imperialism was essentially militarist in nature. The contrast between Roman imperialism —that of a nation of soldiers—and the Carthaginian—the imperialism of a nation of shopkeepers—is patent. At Carthage the economic aspect was a motive; at Rome it seemed an incidental result. Such a result was twofold. The first consequence appears by the end of the Second Punic War. Through the numerous large military contracts of all kinds which it involved, the latter had resulted in the rise of a class of capitalists, whose importance increased during the next fifty years and who appear as a group apart by the age of the Gracchi.

Secondly, in proportion to her expansion in the Orient as well as in the West (Spain and Africa), Rome was becoming a great centre of capital. In the form of booty, war indemnities, and the products of the legal or illegal exploitation of the conquered countries, trade and banking, wealth poured to Rome abundantly. Part of this wealth was scattered among private individuals, part came into the treasury, but did not stay there, as we shall shortly see. In less than two generations Italy became the richest country in the Mediterranean world. For the most part, this capital was not left in Italy. The Italian and the Roman loaned it out abroad, and made it bear fruit by investing it in countries where capital was scarcer. Hence, as the practice spread, the exportation of Italian capital became a factor to be reckoned with by Roman statesmen, whether they liked it or not. Thirdly, parallel with the influx of wealth, the mercantile spirit and the taste for trade were growing up in the peninsula. Many Romans or Italians who had left the plough to go to the war were enticed by the bait of quick profits and transformed themselves into merchants. They bought a ship and set up business with their share in the booty or with the cash realized by the sale of the paternal holding. They are found at Delos by the first third of the second century.

The exploitation of the world which conquest had thus brought in its train therefore assumed the guise of a huge and profitable business from which all classes of the population might draw dividends. To the aristocracy imperialism represented primarily honours, triumphs, provincial governorships, the exploitation of the conquered territory, and speculations in public lands, or, in other terms, power, glory, and riches. To the equestrian class it meant the farming of taxes, public contracts (for military supplies and public works), and banking operations. The profits from such investments were not restricted to the class of capitalists proper, and especially lavish censorships like that of 174 represented a veritable rain of gold for the whole population of Italy. In an extraordi-narily important passage Polybius discloses this as affecting the middle of the second century B.C.:

In Italy there are many works, contracts for which are let by the censors, such as the construction and upkeep of public buildings too numerous to count, and the working of water-courses, ports, mines, gardens, and lands, and, in a word, everything under the control of Rome. The Roman people is in charge of all these enterprises, and almost everyone participates in them through the contracts to which they give rise and the benefits they produce. Some contract for them with the censors, others go into partnership with the former, others go surety for these, and others again pledge their property with the treasury as guarantors.

Let us not forget the peasant who supplied victuals or raw materials, and the rest of the people to whom the policy of expansions meant the remission or reduction of the *tributum*, some share in the booty, regular employment, and all sorts of material advantages. It is, then, fair to say that all classes in the community shared not only in the glory but also in the business of the fatherland. Hence it is not surprising that the economic factor acquired an ever-growing influence on the direction of Roman foreign policy during the first half of the second century, and that, while not yet the sole nor even the dominant consideration, it, at least, lent imperialism the considerable weight it could already command.

SUGGESTIONS FOR ADDITIONAL READING

For the student who wants a comprehensive view of Rome, the best multi-volume survey is *The Cambridge Ancient History* (Cambridge, 1924–1939), of which volumes seven and eight deal with the rise of Rome. A more personal interpretation of Roman history is given by Theodor Mommsen in his *History of Rome*, 5 vols. (New York, 1908), a classic in its own right. For less comprehensive reading, the first volumes of W. E. Heitland's *The Roman Republic*, 3 vols. (Cambridge, 1909) and T. Rice Holmes' *The Roman Republic*, 3 vols. (Oxford, 1923) provide factual background for Rome's rise to power. André Piganiol's *La Conquête Romaine* (Paris, 1927), part of a series of works on ancient history, provides a general view of the subject. Pericle Ducati's *L'Italia antica delle prime civiltà alla morte di Caio Guilio Cesare* (Verona, 1948) provides a more nationalistic view of Rome's early history. The English parallel to Piganiol and Ducati is H. H. Scullard, whose *History of the Roman World, 753–146 B.C.* (London, 1951) is slightly more recent and quite readable. Numerous college texts also exist: among the best are Arthur Boak's *A History of Rome to A.D. 565*, 5th ed. (New York, 1965), Max Cary's *A History of Rome*, 2nd ed. (New York, 1954) and Frank Bourne's *A History of the Romans* (Boston, 1966).

Any text, though, is merely one man's interpretation of what other historians have had to say. The serious student will want to seek out original sources. Livy's *From the Foundation of the City* is available in many editions: Penguin publishes *The Early History of Rome* (Livy's first five books) and *The War with Hannibal,* both in paperback. The *Histories* of Polybius discuss Rome from 220–146 B.C. and are available in abridged form in paperback from Washington Square Press. Plutarch's *Parallel Lives* offer considerable material on the rise of Rome. For those students attracted to St. Augustine's point of view, there are many editions of *The City of God* to choose from, though, strictly speaking, this cannot be considered a primary source on early Rome.

There are many specialized modern studies which limit themselves to one facet of Rome's expansion. For the general reader, Chester Starr's *The Emergence of Rome as Ruler of the Western World* (Ithaca, 1950) is probably the best short introduction. Two companion volumes deal with early Rome, Raymond Bloch's *The Origins of Rome* (New York, 1960) and A. H. McDonald's *Republican Rome* (New York, 1966). Both books are well illustrated and are written for both layman and specialist, but they consider Rome's institutions rather more than her history. Tenney Frank's *Roman Imperialism* (New York, 1914) is a good discussion of Rome's inexorable expansion over Italy and the Mediterranean.

Heretofore we have discussed books dealing with Rome's expansion in general, that is, throughout the Mediterranean world as a whole. But before Rome could expand outside

Italy, she had to conquer the peninsula, and thus Rome's Italian conquest was a natural prelude to her empire. In her early days, Rome was greatly influenced by the Etruscans, and Andras Alföldi's well-written *Early Rome and the Etruscans* (Ann Arbor, 1963) is an introduction to the role these enigmatic people played in the formation of the Roman state. One related group of people inhabiting the highlands of central Italy had to be conquered before Rome could feel secure from their raids: *Samnium and the Samnites* by E. T. Salmon (Cambridge, 1967) is a study of the subjugation and extinction of this people, and Rome's solution to the Samnite problem provides a good case study for Roman imperialism in general. Further treatment of early Italy is given by Joshua Whatmough in *The Foundations of Roman Italy* (London, 1937). Whatmough is interested in the various primitive peoples of Italy in pre-Roman times, but chapter eleven discusses the Latins and chapter eighteen discusses Rome's unification of the disparate elements in the Italian peninsula. Perhaps the best study of early Italy and its conquest by Rome is Leon Homo's *Primitive Italy and the Beginnings of Roman Imperialism* (London, 1927).

Some students will feel that economics is a primary factor in historical causation. The first volume of Tenney Frank's *Economic Survey of Ancient Rome* (Baltimore, 1933) discusses the economic basis of the Roman Republic. Jules Toutain's *Economic Life of the Ancient World* (New York, 1951) covers more ground, but Toutain is concerned with the economic effects of historical events rather than with economic causation. Fritz Heichelheim has published the first two volumes of *An Ancient Economic History* (Leyden, 1958–); the third volume should appear in 1969 and will discuss the Roman Republic. If the third volume lives up to the first two, it will be a valuable addition to the literature.

There are several paperbacks pertinent to the Republic. F. E. Adcock discusses Rome's constitution in *Roman Political Ideas and Practice* (Ann Arbor, 1964). The subject is made appealing by Adcock's dry wit. For those students interested in Roman "culture" and "character," an amorphous subject at best, there are several books of interest. R. W. Moore's *Roman Commonwealth* (New York, 1965) attempts to cover all aspects of Roman life from the founding of the city to the collapse of the Empire. Organized on a chronological basis, Donald Dudley's *The Civilization of Rome* (New York, 1960) is a short cultural history of Rome presented in non-textbook fashion. R. H. Barrow's *The Romans* (Baltimore, 1949) is also short and comprehensive, but Barrow tries to synthesize and to draw conclusions from his material.

Classical antiquity has been a subject of man's studies for two millennia, and it is impossible in so short a space to describe adequately all important works produced even in the last half-century. There are, however, two fine bibliographies covering most of the scholarly output on this subject. At the end of each volume of the

Cambridge Ancient History is an extensive bibliography; the bibliography most pertinent to the rise of Rome is at the end of volume VII, especially pages 909–933. For a survey of the more recent literature, A. H. McDonald's article, "Fifty Years of Republican History," *Journal of Roman Studies*, L (1960) is quite good.